# the
# VIRGINIA
# GIANT

# the
# VIRGINIA
# GIANT

## THE TRUE STORY OF
## PETER FRANCISCO

### SHERRY NORFOLK &
### BOBBY NORFOLK
### Illustrations by Cait Brennan

Charleston London
THE
History
PRESS

Published by The History Press
Charleston, SC 29403
www.historypress.net

First published 2014

Manufactured in Canada

ISBN 978.1.62619.117.4

Library of Congress CIP data applied for.

*Notice*: The information in this book is true and complete to the best of our knowledge. It is offered without guarantee on the part of the authors or The History Press. The authors and The History Press disclaim all liability in connection with the use of this book.

*To Mark Truex and all the National Park Service rangers
who keep American history alive.*

# CONTENTS

# CONTENTS

# CONTENTS

# ACKNOWLEDGEMENTS

O ur grateful thanks to:

Tom Panter, teacher extraordinaire, for introducing us to Peter and provoking our curiosity. We deeply appreciate his insights and inspiration.

Dr. Richard Benjamin for introducing us to Tom!

Mark Truex, museum aide at Valley Forge National Historical Park, for his patient and professional assistance in locating and procuring permissions for the historical photographs throughout the book.

The National Park Service, whose rangers at all the Revolutionary War sites gave us assistance and encouragement.

Betsy Doty for her constant support and encouragement while reading and listening, listening and reading and providing insightful comments.

Everyone else who listened patiently as we talked and talked and talked about Peter.

Cait Brennan, our talented illustrator, for her spirited and evocative visual interpretations of Peter's life.

And our patient and perceptive editors, Banks Smither and Hilary Parrish.

# INTRODUCTION

**B**oth of us are full-time storytellers. With his background as a National Park ranger, Bobby researches and performs historical narratives such as the story of George Washington Carver or the story of York, the only African American on the Lewis and Clark expedition. He also tells folktales, poetry and literary stories. Sherry is a teaching artist, demonstrating the use of storytelling in preschool through middle school classrooms as an engaging strategy for teaching English/language arts and social studies curriculum. We meet lots of interesting people!

Not long ago, we were visiting Thomas Panter, a social studies teacher at Durham Middle School in suburban Atlanta, Georgia. He showed us his classroom, which he has almost turned into a museum, filled with authentic relics from his own family history. Thomas is a "storytelling teacher"; he not only tells the stories of history to his students but also finds ways to help them write and tell those stories themselves.

"Hey, do you guys tell the story of Peter Francisco?" he asked us enthusiastically.

"Well, maybe we would if we had ever heard of him," we answered. "Tell us about him."

Tom told us all about the Portuguese child who grew up to be a Revolutionary War hero. He acted out the battle scenes, filling them with action, suspense and drama. (Wow! Tom's students are so lucky!)

We were intrigued by Peter's story and slowly began to research the legends, myths, facts and fictions surrounding the man. We found dozens and dozens of magazine articles, manuscripts, newspaper articles, chapters in history books, online resources and books of historical fiction. They all agreed on the major outlines of Peter's story, but no two sources agreed on the details.

We began to develop this book, synthesizing all the conflicting information, trying to chart a logical course through the maze. We learned about the Revolutionary War—the details about battles and battle sites, wounds and weapons and triumphs and tribulations. We fact-checked nearly every sentence against at least two sources, and when the first draft was complete, we enlisted the experts with the National Park Service (and Tom!) to read through our manuscript and provide feedback. We assume there are still mistakes, and if so, they are our fault, not theirs.

Peter Francisco's name has been all but forgotten, virtually lost to current generations. We hope that you'll find his story as fascinating as we do and will tell it to others.

Keep Peter's story alive!

# CHAPTER ONE

## WHAT? YOU'VE NEVER HEARD OF PETER FRANCISCO?

Back in the late eighteenth century, he was called the Hercules of the American Revolution, the Virginia Giant, a One-Man Army!

Peter Francisco was believed to have had almost superhuman strength. According to legend, George Washington said, "Without him we would have lost two crucial battles, perhaps the war, and with it our freedom."

Peter's story was published and republished in many newspapers at the end of the war. In fact, the Francisco stories were so popular that in 1828, the early Revolutionary historian Alexander Garden wrote that he "scarcely ever met a man in Virginia who had not some miraculous tale to tell of Peter Francisco."

With all the storytelling, it's difficult to tell where fact ended and myth began, but one thing is clear: Peter Francisco was an example of the strength of the American soldier—those who volunteer, fight, suffer wounds and return to fight again for freedom.

Peter Francisco was a true hero of the American Revolution.

## How It Began...

Like all "super" heroes, Peter's life began in an exotic and mysterious way.

In darkness. And fog.

In the early morning hours of June 23, 1765, an eyewitness watched as "a foreign ship sailed up the James River, dropped anchor opposite the dock, and lowered a longboat to the water with two sailors in it. Then a boy of about five years was handed down and rowed to the wharf, where he was deposited and abandoned. The boat returned, quickly, to its ship. The ship weighed anchor at once, sailed back down the James River..." and into the sunrise.

Peter Francisco had arrived in America.

James Durell was the eyewitness who wrote of that event. He and another Virginia planter had arrived early on the City Point, Virginia dock to check on a shipment. They watched in wonder, the dark, swirling mist making it all seem as if it were happening in a dream. But the boy was real. He sank silently onto the rough planks of the wharf. He didn't cry, just looked around with huge eyes, waiting for what would happen next.

The men called out softly, "Hello? Are you all right?" as the child turned his unhappy face toward them. He stood up as they moved closer, but he didn't answer.

"Son, are you all right?" "Who are you?" "Where did you come from?" the two farmers asked question after question, but the boy remained silent.

Finally he spoke: "*O meu nome é Pedro Francisco. O meu nome é Pedro Francisco. Onde estão eu?*"

The men were baffled; whatever language this child spoke, it wasn't one they understood.

"*O meu nome é Pedro Francisco. O meu nome é Pedro Francisco. Onde estão eu?*"

Peter was rowed to the wharf on the James River, where he was deposited and abandoned.

As the sun rose, a crowd began to gather around the confused young stranger. They, too, were confused. They saw a dark-skinned, sturdy boy with black hair and black eyes. He was dressed in a filthy but expensive linen suit, with a ragged trimming of fine lace at the collar and cuffs. His leather shoes were decorated with high-quality silver buckles, engraved with the initials "P.F."

Who was he? Where had he come from? Why was he here? They got no answers. The child did not speak English, and no one understood what he said except that he kept repeating, "Pedro Francisco." The name matched the initials on his buckles, so the local citizens called him Peter Francisco.

Peter's early life was a mystery, but it was no mystery to the townspeople that he needed food and shelter. At first, the local housewives and dockworkers took him under their wings, feeding him and providing a rough pallet for him in a shack at the land end of the dock. Eventually, though, he was taken to the Prince George County Poorhouse, where he was taken care of while his intriguing story spread throughout the area.

The story reached Buckingham County, Virginia, where Judge Anthony Winston heard it from a neighbor who stopped at Hunting Tower, the Winston estate, on the way back from town. After the two men exchanged news about their families, talk turned to the Stamp Act, which Parliament had approved in March 1765. The law was to become effective in the colonies on November 1 but had been announced by Prime Minister George Grenville many months in advance.

"Tell me what this will mean, Judge," demanded the visitor angrily. "More money for the Crown and less for our pockets, I know that much!"

"You are correct, of course," answered the judge, "you are certainly correct. The act will require that we use stamped paper for legal documents, diplomas, almanacs, broadsides, newspapers and

The eighteenth-century use of the word *stamp* is often confusing to modern readers; we picture postage stamps that were not used until the nineteenth century. The word originally referred to what today is called embossing—the use of pressure on a "stamp" to imprint a raised design on paper, fabric or metal. The use of stamped paper for legal documents had been common for decades in England, and according to law, those agreements made on unstamped paper did not have to be carried out.

playing cards. Naturally, we will pay a large tax for the paper. I have heard that the funds accumulated from this tax will be earmarked solely for the support of the British soldiers who protect us—and that is good. But I have also heard that violators of the law will be tried in the vice admiralty courts."

"And that is outrageous, sir! Matters that go before those courts are heard by royally appointed judges, not by local juries! Those courts will not deal fairly with the colonists!"

"My nephew Patrick Henry would agree with you, sir. He is quite angry with the King, as are many others. I'm quite afraid that riots will be next."

The discussion was one that was being held in parlors and taverns throughout the colonies, but before this one became more heated, the talk in the Winston parlor turned to the Tidewater.

"Did you hear about the young waif who was abandoned on the wharf in City Point? They say he's a handsome boy, healthy and strong, seems to be quite intelligent, though he can't speak a word of English. He must have a story to tell!"

As his neighbor recounted what he knew about Peter Francisco, Judge Winston's curiosity was aroused. He visited the Prince George County Poorhouse on his next trip to City Point, and after meeting Peter, Judge Winston decided to take him to his 3,600-acre plantation near New Store in Buckingham County, Virginia, to live.

At Hunting Tower, the judge arranged for a house slave to care for Peter and teach him English. Most historians say that Peter was an indentured servant, while others believe that he was a slave, but they generally agree that, whatever his legal status, his standing in the household was much like that of a poor family relation. Judge Winston was clearly fond of him and remained intrigued with his mysterious past.

Peter was just as curious as anyone else! As he learned to speak English, he searched the hazy memories of his childhood and tried to explain to Judge Winston what had happened to him.

"Tell me, Peter," the judge would urge, "have you recalled anything else from before you came here?"

"I'm totally certain of only one thing, sir. My name is Peter Francisco. As for the rest, I have only dim memories, as you know. I remember living in a beautiful mansion and playing with my little sister in a large garden. She had dark curly hair, and she laughed a lot."

"And your mother and father?"

"I have a vague memory of a beautiful woman—and I believe she must have spoken a different language from my father. '*Bonne nuit, mon garçon chéri*,' she would say, '*Rêves heureux*.' What does that mean, Judge? Do you know that language?"

"She was speaking French, my boy! She said, 'Goodnight, my darling boy, happy dreams.'"

Peter smiled. It was comforting to know that his mother had loved him and that the language she spoke was French. He was very glad that the words had remained in his memory.

"And your father? What do you remember about him?"

"I think he spoke a different language, sir, but I don't recall any of the words—just that it sounded very different from the way my mother spoke. That's all...all I remember about my father. But I do have one really clear memory, Judge, of the last day I was with my family. That day we had guests, and as the adults were gathering for dinner, my sister and I were sent out to the garden to play. Someone gave us candy and cakes and toys, so we were happy to be away from all the adults and in our own little world.

"We must have wandered far from the main house and deep into the gardens. While we were playing there, some horrible men broke down the bushes—they seemed to appear before our eyes like magic! We just stood there, too startled to react, and they grabbed us and started to carry us away. My sister struggled and fought and screamed. Somehow, she managed to wiggle free and escape. But I couldn't get away from them. They blindfolded me and tied me up in thick, rough rope and wrapped chains around my wrists with my hands pulled painfully behind my back. And they stuffed something oily and fishy-tasting in my mouth so that I couldn't scream. I was twisting and thrashing so much that two of them had to carry me—one at my feet and the other at my shoulders. I don't know how long they kept me bound and gagged—it seemed forever!—but when I was finally released, I was on the deck of a ship, and I couldn't see land in any direction. And after a very long time, the ship sailed out of the sea and into a river, where I was put into a longboat and set ashore at City Point. And now I'm here.

"What do you think it all means, sir?" Peter asked each time he recounted the tale. "Where did I come from? Who captured me? What did they want with a small boy?"

The judge had no answers, of course. What could it possibly mean? He wondered how much was truth and how much was the product of a frightened little boy's imagination. Judge Winston

and his Virginia friends often puzzled over the details, but they couldn't make sense of the story. Many years later, researchers came across records that posed a reasonable hypothesis.

In eighteenth-century Portugal, there was an aristocratic family named Francisco. At one time, the head of the family became involved in an unsuccessful political scheme. The penalty for political failure in those days was usually death, but in this case, a more severely cruel and malicious punishment was ordered: the father would watch as his young son was beheaded! Before the sentence could be carried out, however, the boy suddenly and mysteriously disappeared. Records that would have established his name and the names of his parents have been lost, but the outlines of the story suggest that Peter Francisco may well have been the once-doomed and vanished son. Perhaps Peter wasn't kidnapped as much as rescued. If these records do refer to Peter, it appears that his parents hurriedly arranged for his capture and transportation to America in order to save his life.

Pirates abducted Peter as his sister escaped.

Other records located by researcher John E. Manahan indicate that a child named Pedro Francisco was born on July 9, 1760, in Porto Judeu on the beautiful island of Terceira, in the Portuguese-held Azores. His father was listed as Machado Luiz Francisco, and his mother was Antonia Maria. Together, the two sets of records seem to support Peter's memories, but there is no confirmation that either actually applies to him.

None of this research had been done in Peter's time, of course. All his life, his past remained a mystery that couldn't be solved.

So Peter grew up on Judge Winston's estate, regarded by some people as Judge Winston's ward and by others as his servant. Though he was obviously clever, he was not taught to read or write. From his earliest days on the plantation, he worked in the fields and helped around the forge. As he grew older and taller, he was apprenticed to learn blacksmithing, where he developed the skills and massive strength required to work with iron in the forge.

By 1775, when he was only fifteen, Peter stood six feet six inches tall and weighed 260 pounds of energy and muscle. In Buckingham County, people affectionately called him Hercules, since he was a whole foot taller than most of the grown men and amazingly strong.

# CHAPTER TWO

Judge Winston was a prominent man in the Virginia Tidewater region and a dedicated Patriot. He was well known for his opposition to what he considered British tyranny and often hosted meetings at Hunting Tower, where resentment brewed toward England.

For years, the English king and the English Parliament had had too many wars and too many problems at home to pay much attention to their colonies across the Atlantic in North America. But when the wars and most of the problems had ended, England needed money—and it looked to the colonies as a source of income. Parliament had already decreed that tobacco, lumber and American exports had to be transported in English ships, and it taxed some of the profits on those exports. Most colonists felt that those laws were fair enough.

But they did *not* feel that it was fair for the English government to tax things sold in the colonies themselves. They called this "taxation without representation," since the colonists were not allowed to elect any members to Parliament. They did, however, elect their own legislatures and believed that only those local legislatures could or should tax them.

Parliament didn't agree and had begun setting up all kinds of taxes the colonists resisted, such as the Stamp Act and the Townshend Acts. To add insult to injury, part of the income from those taxes paid the salaries of some of the colonial governors and judges. This meant that the colonists would have no control over what governors and judges did.

The Boston Massacre occurred on the evening of March 5, 1770, when a crowd taunting a soldier in front of the Customs House in Boston got out of hand and the soldier called for help. Captain Thomas Preston and eight soldiers answered the call. The crowd grew to over two hundred people who started to throw snowballs, ice, coal and oyster shells at the British troops. A soldier named Private Montgomery was hit in the face by a stick and knocked down. He fired his musket into the crowd. Then other soldiers fired as well. Three colonists died immediately, and two more died later from wounds. Crispus Attucks, an African American sailor, was the first man to be shot. He fell dead with several bullets lodged in his chest and head. Crispus Attucks is remembered as the first American to die in the colonists' fight for freedom from Britain and the first martyr and hero of the American Revolution.

The colonists protested, sometimes violently, but the protests changed nothing. Colonial anger grew and grew, and the violence grew right along with it. The Sons of Liberty (a protest group formed after the Stamp Act) adopted the motto "no taxation without representation," believing that Parliament did not have the right to tax them because the colonies were not represented in Parliament.

The colonists announced a boycott: they would not buy tea, clothes, glass or paper from English traders. To show that they meant it, the Sons of Liberty staged a protest called the Boston Tea Party on December 16, 1773. They boarded three trade ships in Boston Harbor and dumped ninety thousand pounds of tea (worth approximately $1 million in today's currency) into the harbor waters. Some of the colonists were disguised as Mohawk or Narragansett Indians to communicate to the world that the American colonists identified themselves as Americans and no longer considered themselves British subjects. The disguises also helped protect them from being identified; if they were caught, the men could end up in jail or be sent overseas for hard labor. They could even be charged with treason, which was punishable by death.

The Boston Tea Party resulted in swift and passionate retaliation from Parliament. In March 1774, it passed the Intolerable Acts, which, among other things, closed the Port of Boston. Troops were ordered to move into the city, even into people's houses.

As a historian later wrote, "The fuse that led directly to the explosion of American independence was lit."

Every colony was upset by the new measures of Parliament, and they all sent help to Boston. The First Continental Congress was convened in Philadelphia on September 5, 1774, with representatives from every colony except Georgia. They met face to face to decide what to do in response to the acts of Parliament.

Most of these men did not want to break away from England, but they did want to decide their own future, pass their own laws and levy their own taxes. They explained all this in a Declaration of Rights, which they sent to Parliament. Before they adjourned, the delegates agreed to reconvene in May 1775 if Parliament did not address their grievances.

Parliament's response was to pass still more laws limiting colonial rights.

Now people began to talk about independence. Colonists wanted their rights and would fight for them if necessary. Able-bodied men were forming active militia companies and drilling with guns on village greens. Along with regular militia, special fifty-man units whose members were called minutemen were ready to rush into action at a moment's notice.

Everywhere, people were taking sides. The Loyalists (Tories) wanted to remain British subjects. The Patriots (Whigs) wanted independence. Bitter arguments broke out as neighbors and families found themselves divided.

The men who gathered at Hunting Tower talked of these things and discussed what should be done.

Growing up in this atmosphere, Peter developed an understanding of the growing struggle for independence of the colonies—and a fierce sense of patriotism.

## THE SECOND VIRGINIA CONVENTION

In March 1775, the Second Virginia Convention gathered in Richmond, Virginia. Judge Winston attended the convention as the delegate from Buckingham County, and Peter accompanied him on the trip. The greatest men of Virginia attended the convention, including George Washington, Thomas Jefferson, Patrick Henry, Richard Henry Lee and Benjamin Harrison.

Stormy and stirring, historical in its decisions, the session nonetheless began in a routine way. By a unanimous vote on March 22, the convention approved the proceedings and decisions of the First Continental Congress.

On the next day came the storm. A resolution was introduced by Patrick Henry that drew a clear line between peaceful protest and armed revolution; it authorized action to put Virginia "into a posture of Defence" and directed the appointment of a committee to prepare a plan for raising and arming militia.

This was a decisive measure that, if adopted, would provide no room for retreat. Naturally, it touched off bitter debate. While there was unanimous agreement on the necessity of stressing

Patrick Henry delivering his great speech before the Virginia Second Convention: "Give me liberty or give me death!" *Library of Congress Prints & Photographs Division, Currier & Ives (reproduction number LC-USZC2-2452).*

the colonies' rights and grievances against the mother country, a strong core of conservatives opposed any step as drastic as resorting to armed force.

As the delegates debated, men crowded around the open windows of St. John's Church to listen. It was obvious to everyone that history was being made. Peter was lucky—at six feet, six inches, he stood head and shoulders above the rest, and he could easily see and hear what was happening inside. He was there at the window on March 23, 1775, when Judge Winston's nephew Patrick Henry stood to speak. Peter's eyes grew round as he heard the now-immortal words, "Gentlemen may cry peace, peace, but there is no peace...Is life so dear, or peace so sweet, as to be purchased at the price of chains and slavery? Forbid it, Almighty God! I know not what course others may take; but as for me...Give me liberty or give me death!"

Peter was inspired!

While sessions continued, tempers flared all over town as people debated the future of the colonies and their relationship to the Crown. Peter was reported to have broken up a tavern dispute by lifting the opponents into the air and banging them together until they stopped arguing!

On April 19, 1775, British redcoats marched on Lexington and Concord, Massachusetts; 94 colonists died or were wounded, and 272 British died or were wounded or missing. It was the beginning of the Revolution. As messengers spread word of the conflict, anger and fear raced through the colonies. The message took about two weeks to travel to Virginia. Thomas Jefferson wrote that a "frenzy of revenge seems to have seized all ranks of people."

Peter and other men crowded around the open windows of St. John's Church to listen as Patrick Henry stood to speak.

## THE SECOND CONTINENTAL CONGRESS

The Second Continental Congress met in Philadelphia on May 10, 1775. After Thomas Jefferson arrived in June and took his seat, Congress quickly approved a plan to raise troops and send them to Boston. Jefferson was asked to write a statement explaining the colonists' reasons for declaring war. Congress also appointed George Washington as commander in chief of the armies of Congress; two weeks later, Washington began to create an army of volunteers.

In July, the Second Continental Congress approved two resolutions to send to Great Britain. The first, called the Olive Branch Petition, was addressed to King George. At this time, the Patriots blamed Parliament, not the king, for the problems. In this petition, the delegates expressed their hopes for peace.

The second resolution was the "Declaration of Causes and Necessities for Taking Up Arms." In this resolution, Jefferson wrote, "Our attachment to no nation on earth should supplant our attachment to liberty." The resolution stated that the colonists would fight to resist Britain's harsh treatment; however, they still hoped to keep peace between the countries.

As soon as word spread about Washington's army, fifteen-year-old Peter announced to Judge Winston, "I want to fight, sir! They are calling for all able-bodied young men. Let me join them!"

Judge Winston looked at the young giant with pride but shook his head. "You're still very young, my boy. Wait at least a year, and we'll talk again."

With little choice, Peter waited impatiently. As an indentured servant, he could not do anything without the permission of his master, but he eagerly gleaned every scrap of information he could as he waited to be released from his bond.

The country was at war. As men came and went from Hunting Tower, Peter heard the news of defeat at Bunker Hill, victory in the Battle of Great Bridge and more defeats in the Battles of Long Island, Falmouth and Quebec. Each report of defeat made Peter wish even more desperately to be part of the fight.

He was also frustrated by the reports of soldiers deserting and army recruitment becoming more difficult in all the states as time wore on. Soon after the first wave of patriotic enthusiasm for joining the Continental army receded, recruitment began to become harder and harder. Each of the colonies had separate and different rules about service in their militias. Under the various rules, militiamen were disbanding, going home to plow, plant or harvest. The Congress could not force men to serve and didn't have the power to pay them in hard currency. The Continental soldiers wore ragged uniforms, and their muskets often lacked bayonets, while they faced well-equipped and well-trained British troops. Food was scarce, and pay, such as it was, was slow. But though some deserted, many more remained out of an intense desire for independence and respect for General George Washington.

Meanwhile, opinions were shifting. Thomas Paine's *Common Sense*, first published in January 1776, worked "a wonderful change in the minds of many men," as George Washington put it. Paine argued that the American colonies would have to make a complete break with England.

As minds and hearts changed, leaning toward independence, the delegates of the Continental Congress were faced with a vote on the issue. In mid-June 1776, a five-man committee including Thomas Jefferson, John Adams and Benjamin Franklin was asked to draft a formal statement of the colonies' intentions. The Congress formally adopted the Declaration of Independence—written largely by Jefferson—in Philadelphia on July 4, 1776, the date we now celebrate as the birth of American independence.

Word spread that the Declaration of Independence had been adopted and signed. It was obvious that the Continental army needed every healthy, physically strong young man it could get, and Peter was certainly among the ablest! Finally, in late 1776, Judge Winston permitted sixteen-year-old Peter to enlist in the Tenth Virginia Regiment/Prince Edward Musketeers as a private under Captain Hugh Woodson. His pay would be $6.65 per month, and the term of enlistment was for three years.

Peter Francisco had joined the army.

# CHAPTER THREE

## OFF TO WAR

Judge Winston was fond of Peter and proud of the young man's patriotism. Realizing that Peter's size would make it unlikely that a uniform could be found for him, he made sure that Peter had adequate clothing. Men's clothing during the American Revolution was form-fitted and individually tailored to fit the wearer's body. A suit of clothing consisted of a coat, weskit (vest) and breeches, often all made of the same color and fabric. Peter's clothes weren't fancy, but they were sturdy and serviceable.

Peter rendezvoused with his regiment at Charlottesville, Virginia, and learned about how the army worked—following orders, marching in lines, the various signals of the fife and drum and (Peter's favorite part) how to handle a musket and bayonet.

The men were each issued a musket, a bayonet and a fighting sword (usually a short sword that hung on the belt, called a hanging sword). They were taught a thirteen-step process

People often said that soldiers "followed the calfskin," which meant marching off to war (a military drum has a calfskin head).

Every company expected to have at least one drummer and one fifer. They signaled and communicated orders much more effectively than the human voice. The soldier's day was controlled by various beats of the drum. The nine beats listed in Von Steuben's "Regulations" were the General, the Assembly, the March, the Reveille, the Troop, the Retreat, the Tattoo, To Arms and the Parley. There were a number of signals that were used as well. Beside the beats and signals, the Continental army developed certain traditions and ceremonies. They were Three Cheers, the Grenadiers March, drumming undesirables from camp, escorting the colors, reviewing the troops and for military funerals.

Two soldiers of the Continental color guard playing fife and drum. *Library of Congress Prints & Photographs Division, Frank Blackwell Mayer (LC-DDIG-pga-03961).*

for loading and shooting the musket and practiced until they could complete the entire process in approximately twenty seconds. The sharp bayonets were for stabbing and piercing in close fighting. Peter was pleased to learn that his long arms and extra height were perfect for this task!

The main weapons of the American Revolution were smoothbore field artillery (cannons) and flintlock muskets equipped with bayonets. To maximize the firepower of these moderately accurate and slow-firing weapons, the soldiers stood close together in lines. Peter and the other recruits practiced "dressing" the lines, firing and kneeling to reload as the next line moved forward to fire.

Once the full quota of soldiers had arrived, the regiment marched hundreds of miles to join the main army via Baltimore and Elizabethtown, New Jersey. The Tenth Virginia was assigned to Weeden's Brigade, Greene's division of the main army. The brigade consisted of the Second, Sixth, Tenth and Fourteenth Virginia Regiments.

Transportation in the late 1700s did *not* include trucks, cars, buses, trains, planes or

*Top*: English long-land service musket. *Courtesy of Valley Forge National Historical Park. Photo by Darryl Herring.*

*Bottom*: English socket bayonet. *Courtesy of Valley Forge National Historical Park. Photo by Darryl Herring.*

Once in the army, the soldiers marched, and marched, and marched.

even bicycles. Some of the soldiers rode their horses off to war, but the horses were usually put to work pulling supply wagons or artillery. Most of the men walked.

Once in the army, the soldiers marched, and marched, and marched. They made a thrilling sight as they proceeded through the towns and cities, fifes and drums setting a quick pace and men stepping lively. The intent was to inspire others to join the fight—and to strike fear in the hearts of the Tories.

All that marching was hard on shoes and boots—and feet! Shoes and boots were not as well fitted and padded as they are today; in fact, most shoes of the time period were "straight lasted," meaning there was no difference between shoes made for the right or left foot. To add to the discomfort, stockings were made with seams sewn up the back, causing blisters and sores.

Soldiers sometimes marched twenty-four or forty-eight hours and often more, night and day, without rest or sleep. Naturally, for

On January 2, 1777, John Barstow wrote down the words to a patriotic tune he called "The Amaricans Challings" (The Americans' Challenges), a popular camp song from the Revolutionary era. He might have learned the song from his father or older brother or heard the tune sung by soldiers who marched through town.

The author of the song is unknown, but it was probably composed as America prepared for war around 1775. Songs such as this were sung by soldiers at camps and during marches to boost morale. John Barstow's math book and poem were displayed at the New-York Historical Society in July and August 2012.

In John's words:

*"THE AMaricans Challings"*
*Americans To arms Prepare*
*Honour & Glory Beats For war*
*Exert Yourselves with Force & might*
*Show how The amaricans Boys Can fight*
*For To maintain Their Charter rights*
*Hozah Brave Boys—*
*hark how The warlike Trumpets Sounds*
*Where there is nothing but Blood and Wound*
*Drums A Beating[,] Colours Flying[,] Cannons Roaring[,]*
    *Tories Dying*
*These are The Noble Efects of war, Hozah Brave Boys*

*You That Rain masters on The Seas*
*Shake of your Youthful Sloth & Ease*
*We will make The haughty Tories know, The Sorrows*
    *They must undergo*
*When they Engage Their mortal Foe, Hozah Brave*
    *Boys*
*Display your Collours[,] mount your Guns,*
*Bator Their Castels[,] Fire their Towns*
*You Nighted sons of Amaricans Fame*
*Let not your unDaunted Courage Tame*
*We will Drive The Tories Back again; hozah Brave Boys*
*Why Should we be Daunted at all, Sence we are*
    *engaged in so Just a Cause*
*In Fighting For our Rights and Laws, and dying in so Just*
    *a Cause Bemoved*
*We Will Prove Their Fatal Overthrow*
*Hozah Brave Boys*

Peter Francisco's shoe. *Courtesy National Park Service, Museum Management Program and Guilford Courthouse National Military Park Museum. Catalogue number GUCO320.*

Continental infantry soldiers wearing typical uniforms of 1779–83. *Wikimedia Commons, John Trumbull.*

men in such prolonged and hard military service, shoes wore out rather quickly, but there were no malls or shoe stores to run to for replacements. Shoes were the most difficult item to supply during the American Revolution.

The recruits were vaccinated against smallpox; they were among the first in history to participate in a military vaccination program. The Tenth Virginia soldiers were issued uniforms of blue and red wool "lottery" coats, which had been purchased from France. The weskit (vest) was red wool, and the breeches were blue wool matching the regimental coat. In addition to the coat, weskit and breeches, uniforms included a hat (usually turned up on one or three sides), a shirt made of linen or cotton, a black leather stock (a collar, laced at the back, worn by soldiers to force them to hold their heads high in a military bearing; the leather stock also provided some protection to the neck from bayonet attacks), stockings and leather shoes.

The average height of a Continental soldier was five feet, seven inches. At six feet, six inches, Peter was eleven inches taller than that, with the wide shoulders and thick, muscular arms of a blacksmith. No uniforms were big enough, but he needed to dress as much like the others as possible. Battles fought with black powder weapons produced so much smoke that it was difficult to see more than a few yards, and clouds of thick smoke would form over the battlefield, so it was literally a matter of life and death to be able to distinguish friend and foe. Because the smoke was white, bright colors were used for uniforms. That's why the British usually wore red uniforms, the French uniforms of white and differing shades of blue and the Americans dark blues and browns. Peter's own clothes, plus the uniform tri-cornered hat, had to serve.

In addition to a musket, he carried a leather or tin cartridge box that held twenty to thirty rounds of ammunition, a musket tool and a supply of flints. On his left side, he carried his bayonet in a leather scabbard attached to a shoulder strap. He also had a haversack to carry his food rations and eating utensils (a fork made of wrought iron, a pewter spoon, a knife, a plate and a cup). Add to that a tin canteen to carry water and a knapsack that held extra clothing and other personal items such as a razor for shaving, a tinderbox with flint and steel for starting a fire, candleholders, a comb, handkerchiefs and a mirror. Like most of the soldiers, Peter often stuffed some food in his pockets for easy access while on the march.

At six feet, six inches, Peter Francisco stood head and shoulders above his comrades.

## Peter's First Battle: Brandywine Creek

Brandywine Creek, a small river south of Philadelphia, was the site of Peter's first battle. Only sixteen years old at the time, he participated in some of the day's most savage fighting.

British general Howe's main goal in 1777 was to capture Philadelphia, the capital of the newly formed nation. His troops approached Philadelphia from the Chesapeake, landing at Head of Elk, Maryland.

As the British began to march toward the city, Washington and the people of Philadelphia were certain that the British could be stopped. Washington chose the high ground in the area of Chadds Ford to defend against the British advance. With no bridges, Chadds Ford was the safest and easiest way across the Brandywine River on the road from Baltimore to Philadelphia.

Early on September 9, Washington placed his troops along the Brandywine River to guard the main fords. By placing detachments of troops at Pyle's Ford (the southernmost possible crossing of the river) and Wistar's Ford (the northernmost crossing of the river before it forked), Washington hoped to force a fight at Chadds Ford, an advantageous position.

Washington believed that he had all the fords along the Brandywine guarded by his troops and that the closest unguarded crossing was twelve miles upriver. He was confident that the area was secure. Unfortunately, General Howe had learned of a ford on the creek that Washington didn't know about, and while the American troops were assembling, he marched the majority of his troops in a wide semicircle to cross the creek at that point in the rear in order to launch a surprise attack.

The battle began on the morning of September 11 as the Americans and British exchanged cannon fire. The redcoats advanced in small units, fording the river with muskets and bayonets. An American private named Elisha Stevens wrote, "The battle of Brandywine began in the morning and held till night without much cessation of arms, cannon roaring, muskets cracking, drums beating, bombs flying all around; men [were] a dying, wounded [men's] horrid groans [were enough] to grieve the hardest of hearts."

Historians say that George Washington's greatest single moment of danger during the entire war came at Brandywine, where he was right in the thick of the action. Washington rode his horse within shooting distance of an armed British officer, Major Patrick Ferguson, who stepped out of his hiding place in the bushes and tried to stop the American. Washington calmly turned his back and rode on after stopping for a moment to look Ferguson up and down. The British officer easily could have shot the American, "but it was not pleasant to fire at the back of an unoffending individual, who was acquitting himself very coolly of his duty, so I let him alone."

By noon, the waters of the Brandywine were red with blood. Then, *behind* the American lines, there was an eruption of deadly musket fire as thousands of British soldiers stormed the Continental troops from the rear, trapping them between the river and the overwhelming British army. General Howe's surprise attack had worked: while the smaller British units had preoccupied the American men, the main body of British soldiers had sneaked upstream, forded the river and overwhelmed them.

As soon as word reached General Washington of what had happened, he leaped on his horse and galloped to the point of the unexpected attack, jumping fences and urging his local guide on: "Push along, old man, push along!" Meanwhile, the Marquis de Lafayette, an untried French newcomer to the American cause, was proving his leadership ability, rallying and directing his new comrades amidst the confusion, despite a leg wound.

African American private Edward Hector was a hero at Brandywine. The thirty-three-year-old artilleryman refused to give up and flee. When he was ordered to abandon the ammunition wagon he had driven onto the field, he shouted, "Never! I'll save my horses or die myself!" A Norristown, Pennsylvania newspaper reported, "He instantly started on his way, and…amid the confusion…he calmly gathered up…a few stands of arms which had been left on the field by the retreating soldiers, and safely retired with wagon, team and all, in the face of the victorious foe."

African Americans, both slave and free, served on both sides during the war. The British recruited slaves belonging to Patriot masters and promised freedom to those who fought. George Washington lifted the ban on black enlistment in the Continental army in January 1776. Small all-black units were formed in Rhode Island and Massachusetts, and many slaves were promised freedom for serving. Unfortunately, some of the men promised freedom were sent back to their masters after the war was over out of political convenience. George Washington received and ignored letters from the re-enslaved soldiers. Another all-black unit came from Haiti with French forces. At least five thousand black soldiers fought for the Revolutionary cause.

The British strategy would have been disastrous for the Americans, but Peter's regiment, the Tenth Virginia, and a few others had been assigned to serve as the rear guard. To accomplish this very dangerous assignment, the Tenth took up a position in Sandy Hollow, a narrow cart way bordered by woods. Howe's British Regulars had been pursuing the beaten Americans without encountering a great deal of resistance until they came up against the Tenth. Peter's regiment held its ground at Sandy Hollow Gap for a crucial forty-five minutes, which provided Washington enough time to organize an orderly retreat.

This American stand convinced Howe that the Continental army was still a dangerous force. His troops had sustained heavy casualties, and the Americans, although surprised and outnumbered, had not been frightened into flight. The losses on both sides were tremendous; General Weedon wrote that the British casualties were so heavy "that such another victory would establish the Rights of America."

As the American army retreated from Brandywine, Captain Enoch Anderson wrote, "I saw not a despairing look, nor did I hear a despairing word. We had solacing words always ready for each other—'Come, boys, we shall do better another time.' Had a man suggested, or even hinted the idea of giving up, he would have been knocked down."

Peter had been wounded in the leg by a British musket ball during the action. A musket ball didn't cut its way into its target. It smashed through skin, bone and muscle and sometimes would then bounce around even more inside the body, doing even greater damage. If the soldier was fortunate, the musket ball would pass clean through—a simple in-and-out flesh wound, perhaps damaging some nerves and muscle tissue. But if it struck bone, it was big trouble.

> The Quakers (also called Friends) were opposed to violence in any form. They declared themselves neutral in the American Revolution but encouraged their members to stand fast for liberty and to peacefully resist every attempt to deprive any colonist of liberty. The Quakers raised funds to help the wounded, turned many of their meetinghouses into hospitals to treat the injured soldiers of both sides and willingly took suffering men into their homes.

Once wounded, the soldier's problems were only beginning. He would need medical care, and medical care in those days simply hadn't developed to a point that it could satisfactorily keep up with the diseases, hardships and injuries. Peter was fortunate enough to be taken in by a Quaker family who cared for him and treated his injury. It was there that he first met the young Marquis de Lafayette, who had also been wounded during hand-to-hand combat. While the two young men were recuperating from their injuries, they struck up a friendship that was to last for a lifetime.

On September 26, 1777, the British marched into Philadelphia and occupied the American capital.

Marie Joseph Paul Yves Roche Gilbert du Motier, Marquis de Lafayette, was born in 1757. His father was killed at Minden before Marie Joseph was two years old. His mother died when he twelve, and a few weeks later, his grandfather died as well. He was left a very young, wealthy orphan. At the age of fourteen, Lafayette entered the Royal Army. When he was sixteen, Lafayette married Marie Adrienne Francoise de Noailles. She was not only very wealthy, but she was also related to the king of France.

When Lafayette learned of the American struggle for independence, he decided to come to the colonies and volunteer to aid them in their efforts. He also persuaded several French officers to come with him. In the summer of 1777, he arrived in Philadelphia and was welcomed by Congress because 1) he was volunteering to serve without

Washington and Lafayette at Valley Forge. *Library of Congress Prints & Photographs Division, John Ward Dunsmore (LC-USZC4-6877).*

pay and 2) he represented the highest rank of French nobility. His motives were so patriotic to the American cause that Congress commissioned him a major general. He was not even twenty years old.

Lafayette developed into a loyal and excellent officer under Washington, and having demonstrated leadership in several battles, he was chosen to command the Continental forces in Virginia in 1781. He returned to France in December of that year and went on to serve in the French army. He also continued to advance American interests in France by assisting the U.S. minister to France, Thomas Jefferson, with several economic and political matters.

In 1824, Lafayette returned to the United States and was accompanied by Peter Francisco on a yearlong triumphant tour that included a stop at Yorktown. It was reported that Lafayette was met by "demonstrations of frenzied enthusiasm without precedent or parallel in American history."

# CHAPTER FOUR

## THE BATTLE OF GERMANTOWN

Peter's wound must have been fairly insignificant because he was in action again during the Battle of Germantown less than a month later, on October 4, 1777. The Continental army suffered another defeat in this futile attack on Howe's entrenchments, but there was a lot in this defeat to encourage the Patriots. Though the performance of the militia was disappointing, the Continentals under Wayne L. Sullivan had driven the British through Germantown and retreated only when attacked by "friendly fire." In the confusion of heavy fog and thick smoke that made it "dark as night," according to one witness, "suddenly, in the smoke and fog, [Major General Adam] Stephen's troops encountered a battle line advancing in their direction. They halted, dressed their line, presented their muskets and fired a volley—right into Wayne's Pennsylvania troops." That mistake cost Stephen his command, which George Washington assigned to the Marquis de Lafayette.

Peter Francisco was with General Nathanael Greene on the Americans' left flank. After the confusion of a poorly organized battle, General Greene ordered his columns to retreat. Unwounded himself, the huge, preternaturally strong Peter probably carried and supported wounded comrades, perhaps holding one over a massive shoulder while allowing others to limp along by hanging onto his outstretched arm. The army deposited wounded men in every available building along the roads. Most of the rest of the soldiers from the Germantown battle went on the retreat toward Valley Forge, but Peter Francisco and several others were assigned one more duty before they could encamp for the winter: defending the American forts that guarded the lower Delaware.

## GUARDING FORT MIFFLIN

The Delaware forts were critically important to both sides. As long as they stood, the Americans could keep British ships from passing up the river, and if ships could not use the river, Howe could not be supplied. If he could not be supplied, he could not continue to hold Philadelphia. Because this sequence was so predictable, the British staged an all-out effort to force their way up the Delaware.

The main American defense line, composed of obstructions and the channel-sweeping guns of two forts, was based on Fort Mercer at Red Bank on the New Jersey shore and Fort Mifflin, directly opposite on Mud Island in the middle of the river.

Peter Francisco was among the 450 men assigned to the defense of the only partially completed Fort Mifflin, a post that should have been occupied by at least 1,000 soldiers. From late October through mid-November, Fort Mifflin was under occasional bombardment that was slowly destroying the incomplete fortifications. The men

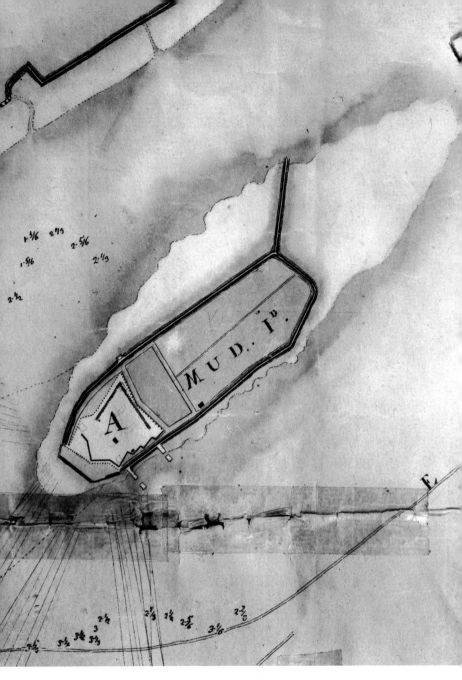

Aerial map of Fort Mifflin, also known as Mud Island. *Library of Congress Prints & Photographs Division, Historic American Buildings Survey (HABS PA, 51-PHILA-111-6).*

were cold, wet and hungry, unable to fight back because this was not hand-to-hand combat but cannon fire. Most of the American artillery (cannons) had been destroyed; worse, there was no ammunition for the remaining pieces.

The men became desperate and creative in their need to obtain ammunition to throw back at the British. Joseph Plum Martin, a private also stationed at Fort Mifflin, wrote, "The artillery officers offered a gill of rum for each shot fired from that piece [a thirty-two-pound cannon] which the soldiers would procure...I have seen from twenty to fifty men standing on the parade waiting with impatience the coming of the shot, which would often be seized before its motion had fully ceased and conveyed off to our gun to be sent back to its former owner." In other words, they were recycling the British ammunition that had been shot at them even while it was happening!

The British attack on Fort Mifflin was one of the fiercest of the war because the fort had to fall in order for the British to maintain control of the American capital. General Howe attacked it from both land and sea. The Royal Navy reduced the earthen and wood fort to ruins, but it took from October 15 to November 16. During that time, they almost buried the fort in mud and dirt by furious bombardment of cannon fire.

On November 10, the rate of attack was increased to an estimated one thousand cannonballs every twenty minutes—nearly one falling every second. This brutal assault crumbled the south and east walls to rubble. Firing continued for five straight days. By day the cannons fired, and by night the remaining American soldiers rebuilt the walls as best they could. Peter's strength must have been invaluable, as he could round up and carry twice the weight in fallen logs and mud as the other soldiers. With his extra height and long, strong arms, he could build the fortifications up much higher than most of the other men could reach.

Despite all their efforts, by nightfall of the fifth day, the palisades had all been blasted away, the blockhouses had been destroyed and the entire parapet had been leveled. During the siege, the small group of American soldiers had held off more than two thousand British troops and 250 ships.

Fort Mifflin experienced the heaviest bombardment of the American Revolutionary War. The siege left 250 of the 406 to 450 American soldiers at Fort Mifflin killed or wounded. Peter and the other survivors carried the dead and wounded to the mainland before the final evacuation. Then, under cover of night, they set fire to the ruins and escaped to the New Jersey shore. Finally, on November 15, 1777, the American troops evacuated the fort. They had effectively denied the British navy the use of the Delaware River and allowed the rest of the Continental army to safely withdraw to winter quarters.

It had been one of the "most gallant and obstinate" defenses of the war. Even the unharmed survivors were almost stupefied from the constant shelling and on the verge of collapse from exposure and lack of sleep. Among the "luckiest of the unlucky," having come through the attacks unharmed, was Peter Francisco.

From mid-November until mid-December, the Tenth Virginia was involved in a number of skirmishes with British and Hessian troops. Then winds turned icy, and sleet showered the men and the pines. Peter and the rest of the survivors of Fort Mifflin followed the whole of the Continental army from New Jersey to Valley Forge, Pennsylvania.

# CHAPTER FIVE

## Winter in Valley Forge

The "march" began in late December under powdery snow. After months in the field, the troops lacked clothing, proper food and boots. Historians say that the men shuffled along, mostly single file, many men with only rags wrapped around their feet to protect them from the winter cold and snow. With wounded men leaning on exhausted comrades' shoulders, it took the weary troops a full week to hike thirteen miles. George Washington wrote, "You might have tracked the army...to Valley Forge by the blood of their feet."

The army of approximately eleven thousand men and perhaps one thousand women arrived in Valley Forge the week before Christmas. It took six hours for the whole column to pass into the triangle-shaped valley, located only eighteen miles northwest of Philadelphia. The day was dismal and bleak, cold, dark, windy, icy underfoot and with gritty snow blowing into the miserable soldiers' faces.

Connecticut soldier James Sullivan Martin wrote, "We arrived at Valley Forge in the evening. It was dark, there was no water to be found, and I was perishing with thirst. I searched for water till I was weary...I felt at that instant as if I would have taken [food] or drink from the best friend I had on earth by force. I am not writing fiction, all are sober realities." Another soldier wrote, "All we have to be thankful for is that we are alive and not in the grave with so many of our friends."

Baron DeKalb, a major general in the American army, said this site could only have been selected "at the instance of a speculator, or on the advice of a traitor, or by a council of ignoramuses." General Varnum wrote, "It is unparalleled in the history of mankind to establish winter quarters in a country wasted and without a single magazine."

But George Washington had his reasons. The British troops had commandeered housing in Philadelphia, and Washington wanted to camp near Philadelphia to discourage further British advances. Valley Forge was close enough to the British to keep their raiding and foraging parties out of the interior of Pennsylvania yet far enough away to halt the threat of British surprise attacks. The high ground of Mount Joy and Mount Misery, combined with the Schuylkill River to the north, made the area easily defensible. Washington also wanted to be close to where the Continental Congress met in order to maintain lines of communication.

Finally, Valley Forge was in a small valley approximately eighteen miles from Philadelphia where the troops would be somewhat protected from the weather. Unfortunately, it was also right in the middle of a nest of Tories who preferred to sell their fresh eggs, country butter and pigs to British general Howe rather than the Continental army.

Washington wrote to the Continental Congress for help: "What is to become of the Army this winter? We have...no less than 2,898 men now in camp [who] are barefoot and other wise naked." He pointed out that the congressmen were in comfortable rooms by warm firesides while the soldiers were living on a cold, bleak hill and sleeping under frost and snow without clothes or blankets. In fact, some soldiers at Valley Forge were forced to have emergency haircuts when they woke to find that their hair had frozen to the ground during the night.

As soon as they arrived, George Washington ordered the troops to cut down trees and dig foundations for log cabins. Thomas Paine, visiting the camp as building got underway, wrote that it was "like a family of beavers, everyone busy; some carrying logs, others mud, and the rest fastening them together." But the men were near starvation and often chanted, "No bread, no meat," as they chopped and hammered. Nonetheless, a neat little city rose on the snowy fields. Not until all the men were secure in their cabins did General Washington move out of his leaky tent and into a stone house owned by a local farmer.

Again, Peter's strength must have been an asset to his regiment. Chopping down trees and trimming

"You might have tracked the army...to Valley Forge by the blood of their feet."

and hauling the logs was hard manual labor in the best of times. While there were plenty of trees to chop down, tools and nails were in short supply. So were draft animals, and without horses, oxen or mules to drag the logs to their hut sites, the men had to do it themselves. With little nourishment, no shelter and inadequate tools, the work was brutal.

By mid-January, nearly one thousand of the huts were finished, but conditions remained horrific. Twelve men lived in each fourteen- by sixteen-foot log hut, sleeping in three-tiered bunks constructed of split saplings. Gaps in the log walls were filled in with clay and mud; roofs were covered in crude shingles, wood slabs or, when nothing else could be found, tent cloth. The huts had fireplaces at one end made of wood and clay, but with only green wood to burn, the smoke was thick and choking. The men coughed and hacked, and their eyes ran. The damp seeped in, making them even more miserable. In the soldiers' diaries, they recorded their running joke: "'Good morning, brother soldier, how are you?' 'All wet, thank 'e. Hope you're so.'"

Surgeon Albigence Waldo of Connecticut wrote, "What have you for your dinners, boys? 'Nothing but fire cake and water Sir.' At night: 'Gentlemen, the supper is ready.' What is your supper lads? 'Fire cake and water, Sir.'" Fire cake was flour and water paste baked in thin cakes on hot stones—in other words, crackers. One soldier complained that his "holiday meal" consisted of nothing more than rice and a few teaspoons of vinegar.

Clothes had been worn to shreds during the summer campaign. One soldier on guard duty was seen standing on his hat to keep his bare feet out of the snow. Waldo wrote, "Here comes a soldier; his bare feet are seen through his worn-out shoes, his legs nearly naked from the tattered remains of an only pair of stockings, his breeches not sufficient to cover his nakedness, his shirt hanging in strings...He comes and cries with an air of wretchedness and

A typical log hut at Valley Forge. *Wikimedia Commons.*

despair, 'I am sick, my feet lame, my legs sore, my body covered with this tormenting itch.'" A New York soldier, Joseph Plumb Martin, wrote, "On our march from the Valley Forge, through the Jerseys, and at the boasted Battle of Monmouth, a fourth part of the troops had not a scrap of anything but their ragged shirt flaps to cover their nakedness, and were obliged to remain so long after."

Diseases spread rapidly: typhus, smallpox and pneumonia swept through the camp. Men weakened by hunger and constant cold became sick and died. Eleven thousand soldiers marched into Valley Forge in December; by the end of that winter, nearly three thousand had died of malnutrition and disease and were buried in unmarked graves.

Hundreds of desperate young men ran away from the misery, but there was no widespread unrest among the troops. For every one deserter, one hundred more stayed to fight again in the spring. Colonel John Brooks wrote in his journal, "In my opinion nothing but virtue has kept our army together through this [winter]. There has been the great principle, the love of our country, which first called us to the field, and that only, to influence us."

Many of the problems were due to a lack of supplies. The army needed ammunition, horses, clothing, proper food and medical supplies, but the infant republic lacked the organization to deliver. When the Continental army was able to get supplies, they had to be shipped great distances, usually by wagon across rugged trails and roads. The wagons were sometimes attacked and taken by enemy troops or by highwaymen—outlaws. In addition to the transportation problems, funding was a constant struggle. The government argued over whether individual colonies or the national government should finance the war.

There was also profiteering. Many American "Patriots" sold goods to the army at outrageous prices; for example, the price of shoes in 1776 was eight shillings (a shilling equaled approximately twelve cents); by the winter of 1777, shoes cost $8; the price eventually went up to $100! George Washington wrote, "I would to God that one of the most atrocious [of the profiteers] of each state was hung upon gallows...No punishment in my opinion is too great for the man who can build his greatness upon his country's ruin." In response, the Continental Congress ordered ten thousand pairs of shoes from France. They finally arrived eight years later, in 1785 (a year after the official end of the war).

Even the strongest men could not withstand the conditions. Peter Francisco came down with a horrible cough and had trouble breathing. He was taken to Yellow Springs Hospital, where he was diagnosed with pneumonia. Peter was kept in the three-story log hospital—the first true military hospital in North America—for two months. The general rule for treating pneumonia at the time was "a large bleeding in the arm. Keep the air moist, and encourage the patient to bring up the secretions from his lungs." Peter's recovery probably had much more to do with bed rest, shelter and hot food than the medical intervention.

While Peter was at Yellow Springs, he was surrounded by horrible sights, the stench of rot and decay and the groans of badly injured and dying men. He was thankful to be released in mid-February to return to his hut and the other men, even though it snowed so hard that week that no wagons could reach camp and rations were reduced from flour paste to nothing. The third week of February was even worse.

General Washington wrote, "To see the men without clothes to cover their nakedness, without blankets to lie upon, without shoes...without a house or hut to cover them until those could be built, and submitting without a murmur, is a proof of patience and obedience which, in my opinion, can scarcely be paralleled."

But spring was soon to come and, with it, a great deal of change.

## Spring Training at Valley Forge

In the early spring of 1778, Baron von Steuben of the Prussian army arrived at Valley Forge. He called himself Baron Friedrich Wilhelm Augustus Heinrich Ferdinand von Steuben, aide-de-camp of Frederick the Great, lieutenant general in the king of Prussia's service, grand marshal at the court of Prince of Hohenzollern-Hechingen and grand marshal at the court of the Margrave of Baden—but the titles and most of the other claims were fake. Nonetheless, he had offered his services to the Continental Congress, which had accepted and sent him to Valley Forge with the rank and pay of general.

The titles were a hoax—he was no lieutenant general, and he had *not* served for twenty-two years under Frederick the

Great—but his skills were quite genuine. He *had* served in Frederick the Great's army, knew his military lessons and had been among an elite group of thirteen officers personally chosen by the great Frederick.

"No other foreign soldier, except Lafayette and perhaps engineer Duportail, so quickly won a place in the esteem of the Army," wrote historian Douglas Southall Freeman.

Steuben was an excellent drillmaster. He wanted to teach Americans to fight like European professional soldiers. He knew no English, so he did all of it in French, translated by French-speaking Captain Ben Walker. Steuben was skilled at teaching precision marching to infantrymen (essential when fighting the British, whose men marched into battle as if they were on the parade field).

Starting with small groups, he taught the soldiers the basics—the proper way to stand at attention, left face, right face, forward march, flank march. He marched the soldiers on the muddy fields from sunup to sundown. When one group was sufficiently trained, he would send them back to their units to teach the others, and then he'd begin with another group.

Steuben wrote and taught an efficient manual for handling the musket, cleaning and loading in ten steps—much more efficient than the thirteen-step process they had been using. He also taught the officers to protect the dignity and welfare of the individual soldier, stressing that it was the responsibility of the officers to care for their men and the condition of their equipment. The captain, he advised, "cannot be too careful of the company the State has committed to his care" and must "gain the love of his men by treating them with every possible kindness and humanity."

Steuben's concern for the welfare of the men was genuine and well placed. Referring to the uniforms of the American army at

Through proper execution of the training commands, the soldiers became a well-synchronized unit. Speed came with practice. In the stress of battle, Washington's men could fire coordinated volleys of musket fire every fifteen seconds.

## The Training Commands

1. Half-cock Firelock: Soldier pulls musket cock back one notch and opens the steel (frizzen).
2. Handle Cartridge: Soldier slaps cartridge box to settle the powder in the cartridges, tears open the cartridge with his teeth and places the opened cartridge under his chin to protect it.
3. Prime: Soldier places a small amount of powder in the pan.
4. Shut Pan: Soldier shuts the steel to hold the powder in the pan and casts the musket about in order to place the cartridge in the barrel.
5. Charge with Cartridge: Soldier dumps powder down the barrel and then places the paper-wrapped musket balls into the barrel.
6. Draw Rammer: Soldier draws the ramrod out.
7. Ram Down Cartridge: Soldier rams paper-wrapped musket balls down securely on top of the powder with the ramrod.
8. Return Rammer: Soldier returns ramrod to its place beneath the barrel.
9. Shoulder Firelock: Soldier holds musket steady on the left shoulder.
10. Poise Firelock: Soldier places musket in the ready position.
11. Full-cock Firelock: Soldier pulls musket cock back to second notch.
12. Take Aim: Soldier levels musket.
13. Fire: Fires musket.

Valley Forge in the winter of 1777–78, he wrote that he "saw officers at the grand parade at Valley Forge mounting guard in a sort of dressing gown, made of an old blanket or woollen bed-cover." The officers had coats of "every color and make," and some of the men were "literally naked." The inspector of the Rhode Island Continental Infantry reported that "the naked situation of the troops, when observed parading for duty, is sufficient to extort the tears of compassion from every human being. There are not two in five who have a shoe, stocking or so much as breeches to render them decent."

Peter and the other soldiers worked hard and learned quickly once they understood the importance of the discipline and the new skills. Before he began to teach the Continental soldiers the new manual of arms, Steuben taught the rowdy men that a soldier's bearing echoed a respect for his trade and attention to the task at hand. According to Steuben, a soldier under orders must remain silent and obedient; he "must not Stir his hands, blow his nose, or much less talk." Within a few months, the dutiful army at Valley Forge was marching with newfound precision and crisply executing Steuben's manual of arms.

It was easier to work hard once spring reached Valley Forge. When the ice broke up, the Schuylkill River suddenly was full of shad. The men took baskets, pitchforks and even tree branches into the water and scooped out the fish, then cleaned, salted and stored them. They ate fish gratefully for weeks.

In February, three public markets were opened near the rear of the camp where local farmers sold food such as pork, turkey, goose, potatoes, turnips, tobacco and milk. The area also housed the artificers' huts, which were a frenzy of activity and the noise of blacksmiths' and wheelwrights' hammers and coopers' saws as the artificers built wagons, repaired wheels and made barrels.

General Washington and the Marquis de Lafayette at Valley Forge. *Wikimedia Commons, H.B. Hall.*

With better weather, Washington ordered the men to punch windows into their huts and remove the clay between the logs, ventilating the smoke and clearing the air. Then new troops began to arrive, along with better food and better spirits. The soldiers marched and drilled hard, slowly becoming stronger and more professional. But they spent some of their time at leisure too. When the soldiers completed drilling and duties for the day, they often hunted or fished to supplement their diet or spent time reading and writing. The soldiers also played games such as cards and dice, whittled, smoked, told stories, sewed or repaired equipment to

"Yankee Doodle"

Father and I went down to camp,
Along with Captain Gooding;
And there we saw the men and
    boys,
As thick as hasty pudding.
Yankee doodle, keep it up,
Yankee doodle dandy;
Mind the music and the step,
And with the girls be handy.
There was Captain Washington
Upon a slapping stallion,
A-giving orders to his men,
I guess there was a million.
And then the feathers on his hat,
They looked so' tarnal fin-a,
I wanted pockily to get
To give to my Jemima.
And then we saw a swamping
    gun,
Large as a log of maple;
Upon a deuced little cart,
A load for father's cattle.
And every time they shoot it off,
It takes a horn of powder;
It makes a noise like father's gun,
Only a nation louder.
I went as nigh to one myself,
As' Siah's underpinning;

And father went as nigh agin,
I thought the deuce was in him.
We saw a little barrel, too,
The heads were made of leather;
They knocked upon it with little
    clubs,
And called the folks together.
And there they'd fife away like
    fun,
And play on cornstalk fiddles,
And some had ribbons red as
    blood,
All bound around their middles.
The troopers, too, would gallop up
And fire right in our faces;
It scared me almost to death
To see them run such races.
Cousin Simon grew so bold,
I thought he would have cocked it;
It scared me so I streaked it off,
And hung by father's pocket.
And there I saw a pumpkin shell,
As big as mother's basin;
And every time they touched it
    off,
They scampered like the nation.
Yankee doodle, keep it up,
Yankee doodle dandy;
Mind the music and the step,
And with the girls be handy

help pass the time. Since Peter couldn't read or write, he may have spent quite a bit of time in the blacksmith shop, helping to repair and make tools and equipment.

Music was a big part of life as well. In addition to the fifes and drums that accompanied the troops everywhere they went, the soldiers often carried harmonicas, small whistles and jew's-harps (a jew's-harp is a small metal instrument played while being held in the mouth while its thin metal tongue is struck by hand). They sang hymns and psalms, ballads, protest songs and folk songs. One of the camp favorites was "Yankee Doodle," which was originally a British song that ridiculed the Americans as backwoods yokels. It told the story of a poorly dressed Yankee simpleton, or "doodle," but the rebels quickly claimed the song as their own and even created dozens of new verses that mocked the British while praising the new Continental army and George Washington. According to several sources, Peter Francisco loved to sing and had a surprisingly high, sweet voice for such a big man.

When Martha Washington arrived at Valley Forge in early spring, she visited the

> Some women went to surprising lengths in support of the Patriot cause. In Pepperell, Massachusetts, after the men marched off to Concord, the women met, formed a military company, dressed as men, armed themselves and patrolled the town. Prudence Cummings, who was elected captain, captured a Tory officer at gunpoint. Later female military heroes included Margaret Corbin ("Captain Molly," 1776, Battle of Fort Washington, New York, wounded and captured), Mary Ludwig Hays ("Molly Pitcher," 1778, Battle of Monmouth, New Jersey) and Deborah Sampson (Continental army soldier 1782–83, disguised as a man, wounded twice).

At the beginning of the Revolution, the Oneida Indians decided to fight side by side with the Americans, thus becoming the young country's first ally. When Chief Oskanondohna received word about Washington and his hungry soldiers at Valley Forge, he sent six hundred bushels of dried corn to the starving troops. Legend tells us that among those who walked the four hundred miles in the bitter winter cold was Polly Cooper.

The soldiers were ravenous, of course, but there wasn't a camp cook or chef. Each man received his ration of food raw and was responsible for cooking it. The corn the Oneidas brought was white corn and quite different from the yellow version that can be prepared simply. White corn requires extended preparation before it can be eaten.

The American soldiers were desperate for food when Polly Cooper and her fellow Oneidas arrived, and they tried to eat the corn uncooked. The Oneidas stopped the soldiers, knowing that if they ate the raw corn it would swell in their stomachs and kill them.

Polly Cooper taught the soldiers how to cook the white corn, taking them through the preparation process and the lengthy cooking time. Polly Cooper stayed at Valley Forge after the others departed in order to cook the corn properly for the soldiers and to help in other ways. She helped feed them and cared for their wounds, and later during battle, she carried water to the troops.

Martha Washington offered Polly Cooper money in gratitude for her thoughtfulness and concern; however, she refused it, so Martha decided to say "thank you" by buying her a beautiful black shawl, which remains in the care of her descendants.

camp hospital, comforted the sick and helped to raise spirits in general. Like all the armies that had preceded it, the Continental army was not just a community of men. Many women and their accompanying children followed the troops throughout the war. They were called "camp followers" because they were usually required to march behind the soldiers when passing through cities in order to maintain a professional-looking army. The women contributed to the soldiers' comfort—they cooked, washed clothing and cleaned the huts. Some even accepted work as nurses. In December 1777, a report for the main army at Valley Forge showed a total of four hundred women present, or one woman for each forty-four enlisted men.

In the summer of 1778, a new army emerged from Valley Forge, better equipped and dressed due to new quartermaster Nathanael Greene (appointed by General Washington on March 2, 1778) and better trained and disciplined. The men were convinced that

Meanwhile, on the western frontier, the settlers were being terrorized by numerous Native American tribes whom the British were arming against the colonists. In June 1778, George Rogers Clark (older brother of William Clark, who would later lead the Corps of Discovery alongside Meriwether Lewis) tried to end the problem by leading a small group of men, aided by the French residents of Illinois, in the successful capture of three enemy positions: Kaskaskia, Cahokia and Vincennes (in present-day Illinois and Indiana). He also captured the British governor of the region, who had been encouraging Indian attacks by offering rewards for every American killed. Clark didn't end the problem, but his mission weakened the British hold on the frontier.

having endured that terrible winter, they could take anything the British could throw their way. More than that, the fact that George Washington had spent the horrible winter in the same miserable conditions convinced them that they could follow this commander to the end of the war.

# CHAPTER SIX

## THE BATTLE OF MONMOUTH COURTHOUSE

Congress knew that patriotism and courage weren't enough to win the war. They needed ammunition, weapons and artillery, all of which required money. They also needed money to purchase supplies and pay the soldiers. To solve that problem, Congress tried issuing American currency, but it had little value and was considered worthless by international merchants. So in 1776, Congress sent Benjamin Franklin to France to request foreign support for the American cause. Though he secretly began supplying gunpowder and arms in 1776, it wasn't until 1778 that Louis XVI signed treaties recognizing America as an independent nation and agreeing to financially support the war. Word traveled slowly of his success, but by the spring of 1778, General Washington was informed that Louis XVI had agreed to send troops to join the fight.

Aware of a decisive American victory at Saratoga in October 1777 and of the promise of France entering the war on the

American side, British general Howe decided that he could not successfully defend both Philadelphia and New York City. Since New York was the better port, he chose to stay there and evacuate Philadelphia. He further decided that the majority of his army would march across New Jersey to New York. He ordered General Charles, Lord Cornwallis, to take charge of that retreat.

When word of the British departure from Philadelphia reached General Washington and his men at Valley Forge, the Continental army sprang into action. On June 19, 1778, six months after their arrival, the army marched away from Valley Forge in pursuit of the British. An ordeal had ended. The war would last for another five years, but General Washington and his men left Valley Forge feeling as though a decisive victory had been won. It was a victory not of weapons but of will. The spirit of Valley Forge was now a part of the Continental army.

After a seventy-five-mile march, the Continental army intercepted the rear guard of the retreating British army on June 28, 1778, at Monmouth Courthouse, New Jersey. The battle that followed has been called the longest battle of the Revolutionary War, and it was one of the most fiercely fought during the entire war as well. Continental general Charles Lee advanced 5,000 men and twelve guns toward the British rear guard. General Anthony Wayne's division, of which Peter was now a member, was in the lead and clashed with a British cover party. Almost immediately, Lee lost control of the situation, issuing varying and conflicting orders and confusing his subordinates. The Americans began to fall back, but when they encountered George Washington, he rallied the fleeing soldiers and disciplined them to hold fast. After fighting for four hours in one-hundred-degree temperatures, the steadfast American troops were left in possession of the battlefield. Both armies suffered equally, each losing about 350 men. Strangely, the heat claimed more lives than muskets or cannons.

Women didn't always stay in camp; they were often on the battlefield alongside the men. They carried pitchers of water to the thirsty soldiers, tended the wounded and more. Mary Ludwig Hays McCauley was one of those women. She married a barber named William Hays at the age of thirteen, and when the Revolutionary War began, William enlisted to become a gunner in the Pennsylvania Artillery. Mary eventually joined her husband as a camp follower during the Philadelphia Campaign (1777–78) in New Jersey and wintered with the army at Valley Forge.

She became known as "Molly Pitcher" at the Battle of Monmouth. Because of the heat, she was kept very busy that day, carrying pitchers and water to the soldiers on the front lines. But when her husband was wounded, she dramatically stepped forward to take over his duties.

Molly Pitcher takes over her husband's duties. *Library of Congress Prints & Photographs Division, Currier & Ives (LC-USZC2-2573).*

Private Joseph Martin, an eyewitness to the scene, described what happened in his journal: "A woman whose husband belonged to the artillery and who was then attached to a piece [cannon] in the engagement, attended with her husband at the piece the whole time. While in the act of reaching a cartridge and having one of her feet as far before the other as she could step, a cannon shot from the enemy passed directly between her legs without doing any other damage than carrying away all the lower part of her petticoat. Looking at it with apparent unconcern, she observed that it was lucky it did not pass a little higher, for in that case it might have carried away something else, and continued her occupation."

Monmouth was a drawn battle. Cornwallis evaluated his situation and decided to break off the action, sneaking away at midnight.

Peter went into the battle as a member of an elite fighting group chosen by Baron von Steuben and General George Washington. He was severely wounded during the battle, taking a musket ball high on his right thigh. The musket ball could not be removed, and the wound caused him pain for the rest of his life.

By this time, Peter's fame had spread in the Continental army. In correspondence to his height and strength, he carried a formidable weapon: a five-foot broadsword, which, according to legend, had been specially commissioned for him by George Washington himself. Peter "habitually closed with the enemy to hack about him"—in other words, he got up close and attacked with his sword and bayonet, a tactic that resulted in many wounds for Peter and many casualties among the opposition.

Peter's five-foot broadsword has become part of the Francisco mythology, and its origins are as cloudy as Peter's own.

*The legend*: Peter met General Washington at Valley Forge, and the general congratulated him on his strength and reported skill in battle. Washington asked if there was anything he could do for Peter, and Peter answered, "The sabers we are issued are too small. They break like toothpicks! I need a bigger sword." Washington ordered that a special five-foot broadsword with a twelve-inch hilt be made for Peter.

*Another legend*: While recovering from their wounds after Brandywine, the Marquis de Lafayette wanted to know what he could do to help young Peter, and when Peter told him that the short sword he had been issued was too small for him, Lafayette arranged for a suitable weapon to be made.

*The facts*: There is no documentation that either of these legends is true. It seems unlikely that such a transaction could have taken place, and it is doubtful that the general would have ordered such a sword made in the first place. It's even less likely that he could have ordered it and had it delivered without any mention of Peter Francisco in his correspondence or account books. Researchers at the Mount Vernon Library have never been able to confirm this story. Likewise, no records exist that indicate Lafayette's part in such a scenario.

*A theory*: Perhaps Peter made the broadsword himself. As a skilled blacksmith, he certainly had the ability, and he may have received permission from his commanding officer to work in the artificers' huts during the long months at Valley Forge to create a weapon that fitted his size and strength.

Although already wounded twice, Peter was eager to rejoin the fight for freedom. After convalescing, he was assigned to the Sixth Virginia Regiment Light Infantry and reported to Middlebrook, New Jersey, in October 1778 for training. Peter was one of a select few who would become a reconnoitering and advance party in missions that required a very different style of combat.

Before the winter of 1778–79, Thomas Jefferson proposed that British and Hessian prisoners of war being held in Boston be moved to central Virginia. A few Tory and Scots Highlander prisoners were detained near Thomas Jefferson's home in the small town of Charlottesville, Virginia. The townspeople were fairly relaxed about the prisoners, allowing them to wander around town on parole. Soon, things changed drastically though—after the Battle of Saratoga, four thousand British and Hessian prisoners were marched more than six hundred miles from New England to the top of a very high hill. No accommodations awaited them except plenty of fresh water and absence of fog. They built a village of huts they called the Barracks. Men from the neighboring county of Buckingham, Peter's adopted home, served as a guard regiment of approximately six hundred men. By 1780, when the prisoners were moved again, only two thousand remained. Historians think many of them were finished with fighting and escaped to settle down to live in the New World.

# CHAPTER SEVEN

## THE FORLORN HOPE:
## THE BATTLE OF STONY POINT

The war in the North was pretty much a stalemate by the summer of 1779, and both sides were eager for a conclusion. Sir Henry Clinton, commander in chief of the British forces in America, attempted to pressure General George Washington into one decisive battle to control the Hudson River. As part of his plan, Clinton fortified Stony Point, New York.

The British position at Stony Point was a protected one, but it was never intended to be a true fort in the eighteenth-century European sense of the word. No stone was used, and no walls were constructed. The defenses consisted of earthen fleches (cannon positions) and wooden abatis (thick tree branches sharpened to points and shoved in rows into earthen embankments; the sharp ends were directed outward, toward the enemy). The defenses were situated on a rocky elevation approachable only from the west, protected in the front by a watery approach and on both flanks by extensive swampy areas.

At first, General Washington was resigned to losing control of the Hudson, writing, "[And] all we can do is lament what we cannot remedy." But after watching the construction of the fortifications through a telescope from a nearby mountaintop and gathering information from local merchants, he formulated a plan of attack.

Washington decided to storm the position using the Corps of Light Infantry, which was formed on June 12, 1779, under the command of General Wayne. The Corps of Light Infantry was a "spick-and-span" elite brigade 1,300 strong drawn from the best in the army—men from Massachusetts, Connecticut, Pennsylvania, Virginia and North Carolina. Peter Francisco was a member of that exclusive group. He was chosen not only because of his fighting skills but also because he set a good example for the other soldiers. Morale was always higher with Peter around; the men gained confidence from him, and older soldiers didn't want to be shown up by the younger man.

In the early morning darkness of July 16, 1779, Wayne turned his corps out "fresh shaven and well powdered" for the thirteen-mile march to the launching point about a mile away from Stony Point. The assault would be carried out in the dead of night, and the men would scale the steep, rocky sides of Stony Point in total darkness. In the inky blackness, it was important for the men to be able to distinguish their own soldiers from the enemy, so each man was ordered to put a piece of white paper in his hat for quick identification.

Complete surprise was required. To accomplish the surprise element, Washington ordered that the men carry unloaded muskets and attack using only bayonets in order to prevent a musket blast from alerting British sentries. The penalty for removing a musket from the shoulder or for trying to fire it would be instant death at the hands of the nearest officer. Until the final assault, silence would be absolute.

Later in the war, General Anthony Wayne was nicknamed "Mad Anthony." Some think the nickname was because he was wild or reckless; others have said it was because he always seemed to lead his men into the hottest spots during battles. But the real reason was his fiery temper.

In 1781, a spy nicknamed Jemmy the Rover was jailed for disorderly conduct. He attempted to get set free by telling his jailors that he was a good friend of General Wayne's, who would order his release. When Wayne learned of this, not only did he *not* order Jemmy's release, but he also said that if it happened again, he would order "29 lashes, well laid on."

Jemmy is reported to have muttered, "Anthony is mad. He must be mad or he would help me. Mad Anthony, that's what he is. Mad Anthony Wayne."

The story spread around the Continental army campfires and was repeated by soldiers in the ranks. Mad Anthony's nickname became a "nom de guerre."

Only two companies of North Carolina light infantry carried loaded weapons. Wayne ordered them to cross the causeway and stage a demonstration attack at the center of the British defenses, where the British expected an attack to come. This battalion was ordered to "lay down a gauling fire" with their weapons as a diversionary tactic—in other words, they were ordered to create a distraction.

The plan developed by Washington and Wayne called for two strong columns of soldiers, one each striking from the left and

The Forlorn Hope struggled
through the sucking mud to reach
dryer ground.

the right. The attacking forces would wade across the low-lying marshes, cut through the first line of abatis and charge the outer defenses of the fort. Once these were taken, they would have to cut through a second row of abatis before they reached the main bastions. At the head of each column were groups of strong axmen whose responsibility was to hack through the wooden fangs of the abatis. Directly behind the axmen came the "Forlorn Hopes," suicide squads composed of twenty men and each headed by an officer. Peter Francisco volunteered for this duty and was assigned to Lieutenant James Gibbons's squad, attacking from the north.

Shortly after midnight on the morning of July 16, 1779, the troops began to move into position. Peter Francisco was the second man in the Forlorn Hope led by Lieutenant Gibbons. The tide was higher than usual, and some of the men sank in the marsh almost up to their necks. With no time to worry about the blood-sucking mosquitoes covering their exposed faces or the strong likelihood of leeches, they struggled to reach dryer ground. Peter's extra height and strength gave him the leverage to pull nearby men out of the sucking mud and help them move forward.

As quiet as they tried to be, the sound of hundreds of men sloshing through the swamp alerted the British picket, who sounded the alarm. The British opened fire from the parapet. Many of the shots went wild, but some struck home. Men began to fall. Unable to return fire because they had been ordered not to load their muskets, the Americans splashed ahead, clambering up the rocky slope onto firmer ground.

They pressed on, reaching the first line of abatis. As the thudding strokes of the axmen rang out, the Forlorn Hope raced ahead. The desperately chopping axmen struck savagely at the abatis, hacking a gap. Lieutenant Gibbons and Francisco squeezed through first, with the sharp, splintered wood tearing and ripping at their clothes and skin. In a furious rush, they stormed the outer defenses, Peter Francisco's huge blade rising and falling in the night. The surprised, disorganized British gave way before them.

With the troops of the left-hand column pouring up behind them, the suicide squad raced for the second row of abatis. Again the axmen hacked a gap, and again Gibbons and Francisco jammed through, slashing a passage for the men behind them. They were in the inner works now, and they swung to the right, heading for the stronghold of the main fort.

The main fort was already under attack: Wayne's column, the stronger of the two attacking prongs, had smashed through the double row of abatis with equal speed. The leaders of its Forlorn Hope swarmed through a sally port and began to lower the British flag; at the same time, Lieutenant Gibbons and Francisco charged in from the left. British troops put up a brief but forceful resistance. Peter's huge broadsword split the head of one of the defenders, and Francisco received his third wound of the war: a nine-inch-long bayonet slash across his abdomen. Before losing consciousness from the severe wound, he killed two more British grenadiers, including the man at the flagstaff who had wielded the bayonet that injured him. Peter lay upon the British flag until he was taken off the field of battle. Of the twenty men from Francisco's Forlorn Hope, only three survived the battle without injury or death.

Captain William Evans, who was there, wrote, "Francisco was the second man who entered the fort and distinguished himself in numerous acts of bravery and intrepidly—in a charge which was ordered to be made around the flagstaff, he killed three British grenadiers and was the first man who laid hold of the flagstaff and being badly wounded laid on it that night and in the morning delivered it to Colonel Fleury. These circumstances brought Mr. Francisco into great notice and his name was reiterated throughout the whole army."

It was all over in thirty minutes—the British were overwhelmed and forced to surrender. In the well-planned and executed nighttime attack, General Anthony Wayne decisively defeated the British troops. The British suffered heavy losses in a battle that served as a huge victory in terms of morale for the Continental army, demonstrating their increased discipline, professionalism and skill.

Although General Washington ordered the fort to be evacuated quickly after the battle, this key crossing site was used later in the war by units of the Continental army to cross the Hudson River on their way to victory over the British.

Peter was taken to Fishkill, New York, where he recovered for six weeks from the belly wound. Though still in pain, he fought at Paulus Hook on August 19 and was reported to have killed two grenadiers with his "medieval weapon." As Peter himself stated years later when referring to this battle, "He never felt satisfied nor thought he did a good day's work, but by drawing British blood."

When his three-year enlistment ended in December 1779, Peter made his way back to Virginia, resting and recouping in one army encampment after another until he reached home.

Peter Francisco's first enlistment had ended, but he had just begun to fight.

Peter's timing was excellent. According to historians, Washington's troops endured an even more miserable winter in Morristown, New Jersey, than they had at Valley Forge. The winter of 1779–80 was extraordinary. When the soldiers arrived in early December, they found two feet of snow already on the ground, and the ground itself was frozen. It had already snowed four times in November and would snow seven times in December, another six in January, four more times in February, six more in March and even once in April. The ice and snow held up supplies that normally would have been transported by road, although sometimes frozen rivers could be used to transport goods by sled. The men were reduced to eating birch bark, shoes and leather belts to survive. Washington wrote, "We have never experienced a like extremity at any period of the war." Lessons had been learned, however: although the winter was the worst of the century, only eighty-six men were lost to disease and exposure, compared to the one thousand or more lost at Valley Forge two years earlier.

# CHAPTER EIGHT

## THE WAR IN THE SOUTH

In early 1778, the British had moved their heaviest offensive activities into the South, partly because they expected to receive support from the Loyalists in the South, partly to recover Georgia and the Carolinas for the Crown and partly because of the American treaty with the French in 1778. The treaty had transformed the war, creating a global conflict between France and Great Britain. When Peter learned of the enemy's intentions, his fierce loyalty to the South and to the newly formed nation spurred him back into action.

As soon as he was well enough, Peter reenlisted, this time in Colonel William Mayo's Virginia Militia Regiment. The militia was very different from the Continental army in almost every respect. Unlike the well-trained soldiers Peter had served with since Valley Forge, he now found himself working with a highly unpredictable and irregular group of farmers and youth—some as young as sixteen—who were unaccustomed to being told what to do and even more unaccustomed to doing what they were told. Since regiments of militia were called up for service by the governor to serve for only one campaign or for "a period of time as needed," they rarely had any formal military preparation. They were often shocked and shaken by camp life and the horrors of combat, both areas in which they had little or no experience.

Militia soldiers were not supplied with their equipment; instead, they were told what equipment they were expected to supply for themselves. Sometimes the weapons and ammunition they brought with them were so inadequate that American soldiers resorted to taking supplies from the British army. Whenever possible, they seized food, firearms, swords, ammunition, medicine, boots and clothing. This equipment was put to use against British troops.

The South, which until this time had been spared the worst of the war, suddenly found itself under severe attack by the British. The British invaded with a fury that stunned the southern states.

It's important to remember that not all of the colonists who fought in the Revolution fought on the side of the Continental army. Historians estimate that approximately 40 to 45 percent of the colonists supported the rebellion, while 15 to 20 percent remained loyal to the Crown. The rest attempted to remain neutral and kept a low profile.

Some historians estimate that at least fifty thousand Loyalists (Tories) fought on the side of the British. Thousands served in the Royal Navy. On land, Loyalist forces fought alongside the British, especially in the South.

Most of the Loyalist soldiers were no better equipped or trained than their counterparts in the rebel militia.

One after the other, Savannah and Charleston fell, with huge losses of men and equipment. The Continental soldiers who were stationed in the South were captured when Charleston was seized.

Congress reacted by appointing Major General Horatio Gates to command a newly raised army to drive the British out of the Carolinas. The army that Gates commanded consisted mostly of untrained, untried militia who were poorly equipped and in need of everything, including food. Gates insisted his command numbered 7,000 "effectives"; however, his adjutant general, Otho Williams, said the number was less than half that: 3,052. For reasons that have been lost to history, Gates chose to ignore those numbers and attacked General Cornwallis's much superior force.

Gates's decision to attack gave the British an opportunity for complete victory. An event that foretold the coming disaster occurred on the night of August 15, 1780. The British cavalry leader, Banastre Tarleton, known for his cruelty, surprised the American advance force made up of the cavalry and infantry units of Armand's Legion, a group composed mostly of foreign volunteers. The surprise was complete. Armand's Legion was almost wiped out, and the attack totally disrupted the American preparations for the battle at Camden the following morning.

## August 16, 1780: The Battle of Camden

At dawn, the full force of Lord Cornwallis's army fell on the left flank of the American position, where Peter Francisco was stationed with the Virginia militia. Few of the Virginia militia had ever seen action, with the majority being inexperienced recruits. The results were predictable. The militia broke under the first crushing blow of the British professional soldiers and ran from the battlefield.

Peter Francisco lifted the 1,100-pound cannon from the gun carriage and carried it to safety.

In their rush, they crashed through the line of the Continentals, creating chaos. When General Gates saw this, he realized that the battle was all but lost and turned his horse, racing to the rear. He did not stop until he was sixty miles away. He was harshly criticized for this action, which bordered on cowardice.

Peter Francisco and a small number of veteran soldiers tried to halt the retreat but with no success. The situation was hopeless. In the bedlam, a British grenadier was preparing to bayonet Colonel Mayo when Peter rushed up and "put a ball and three buckshot," as he later remembered, into the British soldier, killing the grenadier and dragging him off his horse. Peter then offered the horse to Colonel Mayo, who rode away to join his men. Colonel Mayo never forgot the incident. After the war, he presented Peter with a dress sword, which is now in storage at the Virginia Historical Society in Richmond.

Peter was trying to rejoin his troop when he reached an American artillery battery. He discovered that the artillery horses had been killed, leaving a cannon behind to be captured by the British. According to legend, Peter Francisco then unfastened the 1,100-pound cannon from the gun carriage and lifted it onto his massive shoulder, carrying it to safety.

Even Peter was exhausted after that effort. He was resting under a tree when one

**FICTION OR FACT?**
Could Peter really have lifted and carried a cannon weighing 1,100 pounds? People have been known to perform amazing feats of strength when under stress. The United States Post Office found the story believable enough to commemorate this legendary act during the American bicentennial by issuing a stamp showing Peter hefting the cannon on his shoulder.

of Tarleton's troopers came galloping through the pines, taking him by surprise. The British trooper reared his horse above Peter, ready to cut him down at the first sign of hostility.

"Surrender or die!" the British trooper thundered.

"My gun isn't even loaded," Francisco replied, pretending to be frightened.

He stood slowly, lifting his musket and holding it horizontally to the ground—a gesture of surrender. The cavalryman fell for Peter's trick: he reached for the gun. As he did, Peter spun it rapidly in his hands and thrust viciously with the same motion. The bayonet speared the careless trooper and pitched him from the saddle. Peter leaped onto the horse and rode off, but he had not gone far when he found Tarleton's men all around him.

Again, Peter was clever. Standing in the stirrups, he pretended to be a joyfully happy Tory. "Huzzah, my brave boys," he cried out, "we've conquered the rebels!" And so, shouting and cheering like one of Tarleton's own men, he passed through the troop and up the road to safety.

Peter's trick would not have worked if the soldiers had been properly uniformed and easily identifiable, but many of the Patriots and the Tories were in civilian clothes. Often, the Patriot soldiers put bits of white paper in their hats to distinguish friend from foe, just as they had at Stony Point. The Tories used pine sprigs.

Quick-thinking, fearless and resilient, it's no wonder that by this time, Peter had the reputation of being the strongest man in America.

"Huzzah, my brave boys," he cried out, "we've conquered the rebels!"

# CHAPTER NINE

## JOINING THE FIGHT AGAIN

Peter returned to Virginia for a short time after the Battle of Camden, but when he learned that a new army was being raised, he decided to reenlist as a cavalryman instead of an infantryman. Maybe Peter learned from his success in saving Colonel Mayo that his height made him an excellent target on foot but his long reach gave him a definite advantage on horseback.

He acquired a horse and joined a troop from Prince Edward County commanded by Captain Thomas Watkins. The unit soon set off to join Colonel William Washington's cavalry in South Carolina. Just before connecting with Washington's cavalry, Francisco and his companions had an encounter with the enemy, about which Peter himself reported many years afterward:

> We then fell in with the British army of about five or six hundred at a place called Scotch Lake. About a hundred yards from the lake they fortified themselves in upon the top

of a hill resembling a sugar loaf; as soon as he got in sight of the lake, he tied his horse and ran under the bank thereof to discover the situation that the enemy were in, and, after getting opposite to the fort, he discovered there was no danger under the foot of the mount where all of their tents and marquees as they stood pitched, and where there were several hogsheads; and after walking about for some time... went into one of their marquees, threw down one of the hogsheads...and rolling some distance, placed himself upon his belly, with his head under cover of the hogshead, and, by drawing it down gently by each chime, got it to the lake, the British...firing several balls through the hogshead. The British, being surrounded by our cavalry and infantry, they could not come out of the fort. When he arrived at his journey's end, General [Thomas] Johnson and his picquett being placed there, the General opened the hogshead, and the contents were shirts and overalls, and other clothing, which he divided amongst Washington and Lee's men, who were bare for such necessaries; General Johnson himself wore some of the pantaloons. He then mounted his horse and rode around the north side of the mount, where he discovered eight horses belonging to British officers, about one hundred yards from the fort. He borrowed a whip and rode between the fort and the horses under fire, and brought them safe into the camp and gave them to Colonel Washington.

Though Peter hadn't killed a single enemy soldier, he had managed to supply his troop with much-needed clothing and horses.

Supplies were so desperately needed that Thomas Jefferson, governor of Virginia at the time, sent out a broadside requesting help from all Virginians. In his trademark persuasive language, he warned that with the enemy so close, any man who did not support the nation was a "bad citizen." The people offered what they could, providing bacon, oats, wagons, flour, brandy, saddles, bullet molds, guns and other equipment. Some folks made short-term loans of a horse or two; others could spare only a single bridle. It all helped.

On October 7, 1780, the Patriot forces in the South won a great victory, totally defeating Major Patrick Ferguson's Loyalist forces at Kings Mountain at the hands of a gang of angry Appalachian farmers and backwoodsmen. This rebel "army" had formed for no other purpose than to fight in defense of their homes and way of life.

The Tory forces had chosen a spot atop a heavily wooded outcrop, thinking it would provide them with a huge advantage over the Patriot troops. Their plan backfired: the thick woods provided lots of cover for the Americans as they moved stealthily up the mountain from tree to tree. Within an hour after the first shots were fired, it ended. The ragtag over-the-mountain men had killed 157 of the Loyalist force, wounded 163 and taken 698 prisoner. After killing the Tory commander, they treated the survivors harshly, hanging some and allowing others to escape to spread fear among their friends. Then, as quickly as they had come, the angry horde returned home. Their plan worked: many Loyalists began to shy away from supporting Cornwallis. Cornwallis evacuated Charlotte and marched back to the safety of South Carolina.

The victory at Kings Mountain was a great Patriot morale booster. It was a welcome relief to the army when it was still suffering from the ill effects of the defeat at Camden in August.

A week later, on October 14, 1780, Major General Nathanael Greene was appointed commander of the Southern Army, taking command from General Gates. When he arrived, Greene found Gates's Southern Army in bad shape. They were wounded, hungry and discouraged. He went into action immediately, first acquiring

Nathanael Greene was one of George Washington's most trusted and respected friends and comrades. At first glance, he seemed an unlikely military hero: he came from a pacifist Quaker background and was an asthmatic with a permanent limp from a childhood knee injury. But when he recognized that war was clearly on the horizon, he studied military tactics and joined the Continental army. Greene fought at Fort Washington, Trenton, Brandywine and Germantown, gaining the trust of General George Washington. In March 1778 at Valley Forge, Greene was appointed quartermaster general of the Continental army because he was good at gathering and conserving military supplies. He emerged from the war with a military reputation second only to Washington's.

all available food and medical supplies, then reorganizing the Continentals and finally making plans to take advantage of Cornwallis's recent defeat.

Greene divided his small army, sending six hundred of his best and most dependable men southwest under the command of his trusted subordinate General Daniel Morgan, while General Isaac Huger took the rest east. The plan was bold and risky. Morgan's job was to divert British attention and make them nervous and uneasy about their mission; Huger's assignment was to take care of the wounded, sick and hungry.

Cornwallis sent a portion of his army under Lieutenant Colonel Banastre Tarleton to oppose Morgan's attack on his left flank. The two forces clashed at the Cowpens on January

17, 1781, ending in a humiliating defeat for Tarleton and the capture of his army.

Colonel William Washington's cavalry, including Peter Francisco, played an important role in the outcome at Cowpens. Near the end of the battle, Tarleton watched in disbelief as his artillery was cut down by Washington's horsemen. Desperately looking for a way to maintain some pride under the circumstances, he ordered his dragoons to charge, but most of them hesitated to follow the command. The handful of men who did follow orders collided with Washington's horsemen and drove them back for a distance, but the Continentals again pressed forward and finally scattered them.

Peter was in a troop of American cavalry led by Lieutenant Colonel William Washington (cousin of General George Washington) as they pursued Tarleton and the handful of his few remaining cavalry who were fleeing with him. Washington rushed forward, separating himself from the majority of his troop.

When Tarleton realized that Washington was alone, he suddenly turned and wheeled upon Washington, aided by two of his officers, one of whom quickly dueled with the American. Washington's sword was snapped in the encounter, leaving him vulnerable to his opponents.

Just when another blow might have knocked Washington off of his horse and onto the ground, a fourteen-year-old black trumpeter who was devoted to Washington rode up and shot the British dragoon in the shoulder. Immediately, another dragoon took his place, raising his sword high above Washington's head, but the blow was suddenly smashed away by Major Perry's sword.

Aiming with deadly intent, Tarleton then fired his pistol at Washington, but the ball pierced his horse's heart instead, bringing the horse to the ground. At the same time, Peter's group caught up, saving Lieutenant Colonel Washington. The

British immediately turned and ran for their lives, making a successful escape.

Word that the British force had been crushed was upsetting to Cornwallis, but it was another boost in morale for the rebels.

The war in the South was starting to turn. General Nathanael Greene proceeded to wear down the British in a series of battles, each of them a victory for the British in the short run but giving them no advantage in the long run. This harrying tactic was said to be inspired by "Indian-style" warfare, which involved quick and deadly strikes by loosely grouped soldiers who disappeared into the wilderness as quickly as they came. Greene summed up his approach in a motto that would become famous: "We fight, get beat, rise and fight again." By March, Greene's army had grown to the point where he felt that he could face Cornwallis directly.

## THE BATTLE OF GUILFORD COURTHOUSE

British commander Cornwallis was encountering stiff resistance in the South. He had lost one of his best officers, Patrick Ferguson, and many of his Loyalist troops at the Battle of Kings Mountain. At Cowpens, he lost the majority of his cavalry under Banastre Tarleton. With Lord Cornwallis weakened and most of his cavalry destroyed, American general Nathanael Greene decided to stand and fight. He returned to North Carolina and a battle site he had chosen during his preliminary maneuvering with Cornwallis. His chosen field was Guilford Courthouse, a site that would force the enemy to advance uphill against three successive lines of American defense.

General Greene positioned two North Carolina brigades of militia in his front rank with orders to deliver two well-aimed volleys and then retreat. The second rank, three hundred yards back, had orders to do as much damage as it could on the attacking British and then retreat. The third and final line was the Continentals. To protect his right flank, Greene stationed the Delaware regiment of the Continentals with Colonel William Washington's Light Dragoons, including Peter Francisco. The Virginia Rifles were stationed with Light Horse Harry Lee's cavalry on the left flank.

By the early afternoon of March 15, 1781, the entire British army was in position, and they started the attack. The first and second American lines performed well and did as ordered, inflicting great damage to the attacking British. The British then re-formed and drove straight for the American center. William Washington's dragoons charged the British flank, slashing through the enemy lines with their sabers. The British losses were terrible. Peter Francisco was reported to kill eleven grenadiers single-handed. Benson J. Lossing, an early historian, wrote that a British infantryman "pinned Francisco's leg to his horse with a bayonet. Francisco assisted his assailant to draw the bayonet forth, then, with a terrible force brought down his sword and cleft the poor fellow's head from his shoulders."

As the British reeled from the attack, Colonel Washington saw another opportunity to capture Cornwallis himself. Washington launched another attack, but this time the British infantry drove them off, killing and wounding many Americans.

Even though he was already injured, Peter was in the thick of the action as usual. He rode toward a tightly grouped British infantry unit. Peter's son Dr. B.M. Francisco wrote decades later that an upward-thrust bayonet pierced Peter's "right thigh the whole length of the bayonet, entering above the knee and coming out at the socket of his hip." Doubling up with pain, he wheeled out of the action, clinging to his mount in desperation. He rode a short distance before tumbling, unconscious, to the ground—and was spared the sight of Greene's withdrawal, leaving Cornwallis the so-called victor.

Peter was found lying beside four corpses by a kindly Quaker named Robinson who was scouting the field for survivors. The man took Francisco home and nursed him back to health. It took six to eight weeks for the terrible wounds to heal. Meanwhile, his heroism at Guilford Courthouse was the talk of the southern Continental army.

Years later, John Woodson of Cumberland County, Virginia, confirmed Peter's bravery in the battle: "I hereby certify that as relates to the Guilford battle, the above named Peter Francisco did act bravely and was severely wounded. I...was in company with said P. Francisco upon leaving the battleground, and he was very bloody, also was his sword from point to hilt." Peter's huge contribution to the battle is commemorated at the present-day Guilford Courthouse National Military Park, where several of Peter's possessions are on display.

Technically, the Battle of Guilford Courthouse was a British victory because the American soldiers retreated, but it was a Pyrrhic one, offset by staggering losses. The heavy British casualties made it a turning point of the war. General Cornwallis commented, "Such fighting I have not seen since God made me. The Americans fought like demons." It was one of the bloodiest battles of the war.

Once Peter's wounds had healed, he limped more than 190 miles back home to Virginia without money or a horse.

Peter Francisco limped more than 190 miles back home to Virginia.

# CHAPTER TEN

## NOT FINISHED YET!

Peter's astonishing efforts at Guilford Courthouse did not go unnoticed. Colonel William Washington urged him to accept a commission, but Peter turned it down; he felt that he wasn't qualified because he couldn't read or write. General Greene presented him with an engraved razor case inscribed: "Peter Francisco, New Stone, Buckingham County, Va, a tribute to his moral worth and valor. From his comrade in arms, Nathanael Greene." The razor case is on display at the museum at Guilford Courthouse.

Peter wouldn't accept a commission, but he was not finished serving his country. As soon as he was fully recovered, he volunteered for active service in Virginia, where his officers granted him permission to "act however best he might cripple the enemy." This was the only instance on record in the America army where such complete freedom of action was granted to any soldier, much less a private. Peter went into action immediately;

Shaving case presented to Peter Francisco by General Nathanael Greene. *Courtesy National Park Service, Museum Management Program and Guilford Courthouse National Military Park Museum. Catalogue number GUCO319.*

he became a scout, monitoring the movements and actions of Banastre Tarleton and his cavalry.

Banastre Tarleton had earned a reputation for ruthlessness. He commanded the British Legion, a force mostly consisting of Loyalist militia from Pennsylvania and Tory volunteers from the South. At one point, the British Legion grew to nearly two thousand men. It—and Tarleton—was hated and feared by Patriots, and this feeling grew when Tarleton and his men brutally defeated a Patriot force at Waxhaws, South Carolina, on May 29, 1780. A mind-boggling 70 to 75 percent of the Patriot force was killed or wounded, and the Tories were reported to have killed many of the wounded and those trying to surrender. After that, Patriots who captured Tories gave them what they called "Tarleton's quarter"—meaning no mercy at all.

"Scout" is another word for spy, and spies were of huge importance to the Revolution. George Washington once said, "There is nothing more necessary than good intelligence to frustrate a designing enemy, and nothing that requires greater pains to obtain."

The espionage network was vast and varied. James Armistead [Lafayette] was an African American spy during the American Revolution. Born in Virginia as a slave to William Armistead in 1760, he volunteered to join the army in 1781 and became a double agent for the Marquis de Lafayette.

Women used their homemaker skills in espionage work. Both the British and American armies recruited housewives and young girls as cooks and maids, since they could use their almost unrestricted access to soldiers' campsites to eavesdrop on conversations about troop movements, leadership changes and equipment shortages and deliveries without raising suspicion.

Children were used as spies, too, because they could easily blend into the surroundings. One Philadelphia mother hid messages in her son's fabric-covered buttons. The boy would walk to visit the camp where his older brother was a soldier and then "happen" to lose his button, which his brother would "happen" to find; the button contained notes on British plans of attack.

Even Benjamin Franklin was a spy. He was sent over to England on several occasions to spy out the actions of Parliament. Because of his family's loyalty to the Crown, he could get in and out of there without suspicion.

Peter had already met up with Tarleton's troops at Camden, of course, and had developed a personal bitterness toward them. One day in July 1781, he was sitting quietly in the inn yard of Benjamin Ward's house (also known as Ward's Tavern) in Amelia County, Virginia, with a mug of ale. Nine of Tarleton's troopers suddenly galloped up along the road and surrounded him. Peter didn't have time to escape. Being Peter, he probably didn't want to. He stood quietly like a man submitting to his fate.

Eight of the troopers went inside the tavern, but one approached Peter with his saber drawn. The conversation, as historian Alexander Garden later related it (maybe with some enhancement of his own), went like this:

"Give up instantly and surrender everything you have of value or prepare to die!" the trooper thundered.

"I have nothing to give up," said Francisco with a shrug.

"So use your pleasure."

The dragoon's greedy eyes were drawn to a pair of large silver buckles that Peter wore on his shoes. These were not the expensive "P.F." buckles that he had worn as a boy when he arrived at City Point; those had been left with Judge Winston's wife for safekeeping. The judge had replaced them with the plainer but expensive silver buckles that caught the eye of the British trooper.

"Give me instantly those silver buckles on your shoes," the cavalryman ordered, waving his sword.

"They were a present to me from a valued friend," Peter replied calmly. "Give them up, I never will. You have the power. Take them if you see fit."

The cavalryman foolishly thought it was an invitation. He tucked his saber beneath his arm and stooped to yank the buckles from Peter's shoes. Bending over, he inadvertently presented his saber to Peter, hilt first and sheathed beneath his armpit. Quickly, Peter grabbed the saber by the hilt, wrenched it free and, in almost the same sweeping motion, delivered one of those awesome Francisco strokes. He split the trooper's head and neck in half down to his shoulders.

The commotion alerted the other eight troopers, who came rushing from the tavern. One aimed a pistol at Francisco. Peter sprang at him with the saber. The dragoon fired just as Peter swung the saber. The shot grazed Francisco's side, while the saber practically severed the hand that had fired the shot. With another blow, Francisco cut down the trooper.

Meanwhile, another of the dragoons mounted his horse. Ben Ward, the tavern keeper, had come running into the yard with the dragoons. He grabbed a musket and passed it up to the mounted soldier.

The trooper aimed the musket at Peter's chest and pulled the trigger. It misfired. Immediately, Peter reached up, grabbed the musket, wrenched it from the dragoon's hands and clubbed him from the saddle. Then Peter leaped onto the horse, rose in the stirrups and yelled, "Come on, my brave boys, now's your time; let's dispatch these few!"

Peter charged just as if he really were at the head of a large troop. When he cut down another of the soldiers, the rest of the squad broke and ran in panic across the fields.

Peter whirled on the tavern keeper who had nearly cost him his life.

"I seized Ward and would have dispatched him," Francisco reported afterward, "but the poor wretch begged for his life. He was not only an object of my contempt, but pity. The eight horses that were left behind I gave him to conceal for me."

The soldiers who had escaped rejoined Tarleton, who was about a mile off. Tarleton and his four-hundred-man force rushed to the scene. Ten of them broke out in front of the rest, riding to cut Peter off, but he spurred his captured horse and took off down an obscure country road. Using his knowledge of the countryside, he easily eluded his pursuers.

The next day, although Tarleton's troop was still in the vicinity, Francisco rode back to the tavern and retrieved six of the captured horses from Ward. He kept the best horse for himself, and in memory of the way he had acquired the animal, he renamed it Tarleton. He sold the other horses at the Prince Edward Courthouse the following day and turned the funds over to the government. Tarleton became Peter's favorite horse, which he rode for years afterward.

The "battle at Ward's Tavern" became one of the best-known anecdotes told about Peter Francisco after the war. In 1814, the artist James Worrell painted an imaginative re-creation of the scene that was hung in Independence Hall in Philadelphia.

Soon after this incident, Peter reconnected with Lafayette, serving as the Frenchman's aide and companion.

# CHAPTER ELEVEN

## SURRENDER AT YORKTOWN

Rather than an all-out attack on Cornwallis, General Nathanael Greene used hit-and-run tactics to inflict damage on the British. This guerrilla warfare managed to drive the British toward the coast and back to Yorktown.

The need to move quickly required the British troops to lighten their load. To do so, the soldiers were ordered to strip themselves of all excess baggage, including tents. Now lacking shelter, they adopted housing strategies from the local Native Americans. One officer with the Seventy-sixth Regiment later wrote about Cornwallis's 1781 campaign in Virginia, "Our encampments were always chosen on the banks of a stream, and were extremely picturesque, as we had no tents, and were obliged to construct wigwams of fresh boughs to keep off the rays of the sun during the day." Wigwams could be quickly and easily built from materials at hand, made fairly waterproof and left behind when the army moved on.

At the same time that General Charles Cornwallis and the British army were retreating to Yorktown, General George Washington was marching his army down from the north. Meanwhile, the French navy started to move twenty-four ships of the line—nearly a quarter of its fleet—into position on the Virginia coast.

On September 5, 1781, the French fleet attacked and defeated the British navy in Chesapeake Bay. French admiral de Grass then repositioned his fleet and began bombarding the forts where Cornwallis and his troops were stationed at Yorktown.

Sergeant Joseph Martin was a member of the new engineer corps, the Sappers and Miners. Among the corps' principal duties was building trenches and fortifications. In the summer of 1781, Martin was stationed near Yorktown, Virginia, where he and his men were working through the night. In the near-total darkness, he saw a tall man reach for a pickaxe and begin to dig part of a trench. He later learned that he was working alongside General George Washington! Not only did Washington dig in the trenches, but he was also often seen close to the open fighting, taking risk after risk. One time a cannonball struck so close by that it covered his companion's hat with sand.

The Siege of Yorktown was effective. Cornwallis was trapped between the American army and the French navy. For eleven days, the American forces bombarded the British. By mid-October, Cornwallis was running out of food and ammunition. His troops were suffering from disease, horrible weather and a failed evacuation. It was time to surrender.

On October 17, 1781, Cornwallis sent out a white flag. Ensign Ebenezer Denny of Connecticut wrote:

> [This morning we]...had the pleasure of seeing a drummer mount the enemy's parapet, and beat a parley, and immediately an officer, holding up a white handkerchief, made his

> appearance outside their works; the drummer accompanied
> him, beating. Our batteries ceased. An officer from our lines
> ran and met the other, and tied the handkerchief over his eyes.
> The drummer sent back, and the British officer conducted to
> a house in rear of our lines. Firing ceased totally.

The blindfolded Englishman carried a memorandum from Cornwallis to Washington reading, "I propose a cessation of hostilities for 24 hours, and that two officers may be appointed by each side, to meet at Mr. Moore's house, to settle the terms for the surrender of York and Gloucester." Gloucester was the British stronghold on the north shore of York River, opposite Yorktown.

Washington responded that he would allow Cornwallis two hours to put his proposals in writing, and among other things, he said, "The same Honors will be granted to the Surrendering Army as were granted to the Garrison of Charles Town." (Benjamin Lincoln, who was now Washington's second in command, had been the defeated commander at Charleston in 1780. Eighteenth-century customs of war usually gave the surrendering commander the honor of allowing him to march out of his lines to lay down his arms with his flags flying and his band playing a march from the victor's national book of martial melodies. But Clinton dishonored Lincoln by requiring the Americans to keep their colors cased and forbidding them to play an English or German melody. Washington was letting Cornwallis know that the British were going to be treated exactly the same way.)

It was agreed that both sides would send representatives the next morning to Augustine Moore's house to commit the terms to paper. Lieutenant Colonel Thomas Dundas and Major Alexander Ross, representing Cornwallis, negotiated the details with Lieutenant Colonel John Laurens, representing the

Americans, and Viscount de Noailles, representing America's ally, the French, commanded by the Count de Rochambeau.

The British nitpicked over every provision. The negotiations, which Washington expected to be concluded by noon, took all day. At one point, Ross told Laurens, who had been with Lincoln at Charleston, that a passage in Article Three was harsh. It read, "The garrison of York will march out to a place to be appointed in front of his posts, at two o'clock precisely, with shouldered arms, colors cased, and drums beating a British or German march."

"Yes, sir," Laurens said, "it is a harsh article." Ross said that since Clinton, not Cornwallis, had been responsible for the insult to Benjamin Lincoln, Article Three was unfair. Laurens said, "This remains an article or I cease to be a commissioner."

While three armies waited for the four-man discussion to conclude, Denny wrote, "Several flags pass and repass now even without the drum. Had we not seen the drummer in his red coat when he first mounted, he might have beat away till doomsday. The constant firing was too much for the sound of a single drum; but when the firing ceased, I thought I never heard a drum equal to it—the most delightful music to us all."

American brigadier general Henry Knox wrote that day to his wife, "They will have the same *honors* as the garrison of Charleston; that is they will *not* be permitted to unfurl their colors or play *Yankee Doodle*."

Although Peter's name appears on the rolls of those who fought at Yorktown, it's not clear whether he actually did fight. It is clear, however, that he was granted the supreme satisfaction of being present when Cornwallis surrendered.

Here is what Peter saw on October 19, 1781, in the words of Dr. James Thacher, who served with the Continental army and published his account of the surrender several years later:

At about twelve o'clock, the combined army was arranged and drawn up in two lines extending more than a mile in length. The Americans were drawn up in a line on the right side of the road, and the French occupied the left. At the head of the former, the great American commander [George Washington], mounted on his noble courser, took his station, attended by his aides. At the head of the latter was posted the excellent Count Rochambeau and his suite. The French troops, in complete uniform, displayed a martial and noble appearance; their bands of music, of which the timbrel formed a part, is a delightful novelty, and produced while marching to the ground a most enchanting effect.

The Americans, though not all in uniform, nor their dress so neat, yet exhibited an erect, soldierly air, and every countenance beamed with satisfaction and joy. The concourse of spectators from the country was prodigious, in point of numbers was probably equal to the military, but universal silence and order prevailed.

It was about two o'clock when the captive army advanced through the line formed for their reception. Every eye was prepared to gaze on Lord Cornwallis, the object of peculiar interest and solicitude; but he disappointed our anxious expectations; pretending indisposition, he made General O'Hara his substitute as the leader of his army. This officer was followed by the conquered troops in a slow and solemn step, with shouldered arms, colors cased and drums beating a British march. Having arrived at the head of the line, General O'Hara, elegantly mounted, advanced to his excellency the commander-in-chief, taking off his hat, and apologized for the non-appearance of Earl Cornwallis. With his usual dignity and politeness, his excellency pointed to Major-General Lincoln for directions, by whom the British army was conducted into a spacious field, where it was intended they should ground their arms.

The royal troops, while marching through the line formed by the allied army, exhibited a decent and neat appearance, as respects arms and clothing, for their commander opened his store and directed every soldier to be furnished with a new suit complete, prior to the capitulation. But in their line of march we remarked a disorderly and unsoldierly conduct, their step was irregular, and their ranks frequently broken.

But it was in the field, when they came to the last act of the drama, that the spirit and pride of the British soldier was put to the severest test: here their mortification could not be concealed. Some of the platoon officers appeared to be exceedingly chagrined when giving the word "*ground arms*," and I am a witness that they performed this duty in a very unofficer-like manner; and that many of the soldiers manifested a *sullen temper*, throwing their arms on the pile with violence, as if determined to render them useless. This irregularity, however, was checked by the authority of General Lincoln. After having grounded their arms and divested themselves of their accoutrements, the captive troops were conducted back to Yorktown and guarded by our troops till they could be removed to the place of their destination.

According to legend, when General Cornwallis and his British troops marched out of Yorktown with their drums covered with black handkerchiefs, they played a tune called "The World Turned Upside Down." The legend doesn't seem to have any proof behind it, but the song clearly represented the way the British felt. It included verses such as:

If ponies rode men and grass ate horses,
And cats were chased in to holes by the mouse;
If summer were spring and the other way round,
Then all the world would be upside down.

Certainly, Great Britain's world had been turned upside down. The unsophisticated forces of America had defeated the most powerful country in Europe.

Although the war continued in the Atlantic and a few other sites, the Patriot victory at Yorktown effectively ended fighting in the American colonies. Peace negotiations began in 1782, and on September 3, 1783, the Treaty of Paris was signed, formally recognizing the United States as a free and independent nation after eight years of war.

# CHAPTER TWELVE

## WHEN THE BATTLES ENDED

After the surrender at Yorktown, Peter returned to the Hunting Tower plantation, but for unknown reasons, the relationship between Francisco and Judge Winston had become tense and awkward. Peter left the estate after the war and never returned.

According to family tradition, Peter Francisco returned to Richmond with Lafayette soon after the surrender at Yorktown, and while strolling in front of St. John's Church (the same place Peter had heard Patrick Henry's famous "Give me liberty" speech), the two young men saw a young woman trip. Before she could fall, she was caught by Peter. That was the way he met Susannah Anderson.

Perhaps it was love at first sight. Peter wanted to marry sixteen-year-old Susannah Anderson, who was the daughter of James Anderson of the Mansion estate in Cumberland County. Susannah's family did not approve of a match between the two, mostly because Francisco was still illiterate and had no money. Peter decided to remove the obstacles to his happiness.

He began by opening a small store and tavern on the Willis River at New Store in Buckingham County. He also set up a blacksmith shop on a piece of land that was given to him by Joseph Curd, an army comrade. Once he was earning some money, Peter went to school.

At the age of twenty-six, six-foot, six-inch Peter Francisco enrolled in a neighborhood school to learn to read and write. The other students loved hearing his stories about the war, and of course, the gentle giant stood out among the schoolchildren. They must have enjoyed teasing him about his immense size! It's easy to picture Peter sitting on the low benches with his knees up around his ears. He must have been an excellent student, though, because within three years, he was reading the classics.

Frank McGraw, who ran the school, enjoyed his enormous student. He wrote, "Francisco could take me in his right hand and pass me over the room, playing my head against the ceiling as though I had been a doll. My weight was one hundred and ninety pounds. He evidently inherited eloquence...and he possessed the rare but simple formula of originality and directness. His ability was striking, his personality charming. He possessed a high sense of honor and vast physical courage with a gentleness whose foundation was fixed."

In 1784, when he was twenty-four years old, Peter Francisco married Susannah Anderson.

With marriage, Peter Francisco became prosperous. Susannah apparently brought as her dowry an estate called Locust Grove, near Richmond, Virginia, where Peter lived out his life. He acquired slaves and property and became a planter and country gentleman. Although he wasn't Virginia gentry, he was most likely among the better-off residents of the county at the time. With money and leisure, he indulged his newly acquired taste for learning, avidly reading ancient and modern history and treating his books as carefully as treasures.

Book learning certainly didn't make Peter any weaker. In December 1784, Samuel Shepard wrote about Peter in his diary:

> I watched the blacksmith at his work and never before saw muscles as great and developed in so young a man, or boy, he is still a boy. I usually write about a man's face. Of this smith I noticed first his great hands, long broad the fingers square, the thumbs heavy and larger in the nail than the usual great toe. His feet are exceptional for length and thickness as is his whole body. His shoulders like some old statue, like a figure of Michaelangelo's imagination like his Moses but not like his David. His jaw is long, heavy, the nose powerful, the slant forehead partly concealed by uncombed black hair of a shaggy aspect. His voice was light, surprising me as if a bull should bellow in a whisper. His eyes very friendly and kind. He talked of the war, eagerly told me of stealing clothes from under the enemy guns, all with humor.

Peter liked to dress well, wearing high hats, silk stockings and bright waistcoats. He became, in the words of an acquaintance, "a product of the social influence of Virginia, and as charming as those who know they are descended from England's royalty." Not surprising, since research indicates that he may actually have been descended from Portuguese nobility.

## Tall Tales or True?

While Peter was evolving into a gentleman, he remained true to himself and his reputation as the Colossus of the Continental Line. Whenever superhuman strength was needed in order to perform a task, Peter Francisco always seemed equal to the challenge. As the years passed, his tremendous physique continued to supply enough power for almost any job.

People shared folkloric tales about Francisco's strength during his lifetime and for many generations to come, and it's difficult to separate the fact from the fiction. Following are some of the tall tales—or true tales—that have survived to this day.

## The Milk Cow

Neighbors once sent for Peter Francisco to come to a swampy meadow. When he arrived, he found a milk cow and her calf stuck in the mud, both mooing miserably. Francisco yanked the one-thousand-pound cow out of the mud with a squelching plop and wedged her under one arm. Then, with only one arm free, he pulled the calf out and held it under his other arm. With the cattle safely in his grasp, he waded out of the mud, hauling them both to firm ground.

## Six Mules and a Wagon

One wintry day, Peter was traveling on a muddy highway when he came upon a heavily loaded tobacco wagon stalled in the swamp. Three teams of mules were unsuccessfully straining to move it. After telling the driver to unhitch the mules, Francisco put his shoulders against the rear of the wagon, heaved and lifted it out of the marsh, accomplishing what six mules had failed to do.

## Toys in His Hands

At gatherings, Peter often lifted two 160-pound men, one in either hand, straight up to the ceiling. Maybe the habit started with his schoolteacher, who must have spread the word that Peter could lift him like a toy in his hands.

## Peter and the Carpenter

Peter Francisco hired a carpenter to shingle the roof of his barn, but he was dissatisfied with the quality of the work and scolded the carpenter. The carpenter, a medium-sized man (probably five feet, four inches or so), was infuriated by the complaint, so he charged down off the roof, ready to fight. Francisco simply stretched out his huge hands, grabbed the angry carpenter by the neck and breeches and heaved. The carpenter flew through the air and landed right back on the roof of the barn. It must have been quite a surprise to find himself flying through the air and ending up exactly where he'd started! Once he collected his wits and pulled himself together, the astonished man looked down at Francisco and shouted, "Well, you can whip me maybe, but I'll be damned if you can skeer me!"

## The Prize Beam

Peter was having a tobacco barn built on his place, and a prize beam was needed. He sent some of his servants to the woods to cut one. They returned eventually with an average-sized beam. Peter Francisco looked at it and said, "I want a prize beam, not a walking cane. Go get another!"

Again the men returned, this time with the announcement that a prize beam had been cut but the men could not get it to the barn, as it was too large to handle.

"All right, we will go for it," said Peter. When he reached the woods, he told the men to get hold of the small end of the beam and he would carry the large end, which he did with the greatest of ease.

Such anecdotes, elaborated and enlarged upon as they were told, spread Peter Francisco's fame far and wide throughout the states and territories. They also made him a marked man at a time in American history when there was great significance placed on physical strength. In a booming frontier society, the virtues of courage and strength, the ability to work and the willingness to dare counted heavily. Inevitably, male pride set an exaggerated value on sheer muscle, and the mere existence of a reputed Hercules like Peter Francisco was a challenge to other strong men who were unwilling to acknowledge that anyone could be superior to them. The result was that the more incredible and fantastic tales they had heard about Peter, the more the bullies wanted to confront him. They came seeking "trial by sinew."

## Two Mighty (Stupid) Men

Two farmers from a nearby county, both mighty men in their own opinions, began bragging in a local tavern: "We can whip any man in this county—no, any man in Virginia!"

The barkeeper laughed. "There is a man right here in Buckingham County who could handle both of you with one hand tied behind his back! Trouble is, you see, Peter's a peaceable fellow. Won't be easy to get him riled enough to fight you."

The big, strong farmers, full of too much alcohol, sneered at this. "We'll get your Samson to fight all right!" they bragged, and they bet $100 that they could not only provoke a fight but win it. The barkeeper must have been eager to make that bet.

It wasn't long before Peter walked quietly into the tavern, innocent and unsuspecting. The barkeep nodded in his direction, indicating he was the man, and the two farmers slinked up behind Francisco. He had gone straight to the fire to warm himself and was just lowering himself into a chair when one of the strangers yanked the chair away. Francisco fell heavily, and they jumped on him.

Big mistake! Peter shook them off the way a dog shakes off water. He rose to his feet roaring like an injured bear. He reached out his two huge hands, grabbed each of the would-be bullies by the nape of the neck, yanked them off their feet and cracked their heads together with almost skull-splitting force. Both men were knocked unconscious, and he dumped them limply on the floor. One woke up late in the afternoon, and the other remained unconscious until the next day.

## Mr. Pamphlet

When politician Henry Clay visited Peter Francisco in 1826, he was very impressed by the still mighty muscles of the Revolutionary warrior. Clay asked Peter if he had ever met his match in a test of strength.

Francisco said he never had and, laughing, told a story about a man who had traveled all the way from Clay's native Kentucky to match strength with him.

"Your Kentucky strong-man was named Pamphlet," Francisco recalled, "and this incident occurred while I was working at my tavern at New Store. I was in the yard outside the tavern when this man Pamphlet rode up, asking for Peter Francisco.

"'I've come all the way from Kentucky just to whip him!' he told me.

"I just smiled and called a servant and sent him to cut some willow switches. Then I presented the switches to Mr. Pamphlet and turned my back.

"'Whip away, sir, so that you can go back to Kentucky and say you have carried out your boast!'

"Well, sir, Pamphlet seemed to resent my attitude! He insisted on trying to lift me. Finally, I submitted in order to get it over with, and the man hoisted me up and down several times—none too gently! Finally, he acknowledged that I was indeed a mighty heavy man.

"'All right, Mr. Pamphlet,' I said, 'you've felt my weight. Now let me feel yours.'

"I took hold of Pamphlet, lifted him twice into the air and then tossed him lightly over a four-foot fence into the dust of the roadway.

"Pamphlet seemed astonished—hardly able to believe that he was where he was, lying in the dirt of the road. He looked up and remarked in a half-sarcastic tone that if I would throw his horse over the fence, too, he would go away convinced. To be obliging, I led the horse to the fence, put my left arm across the horse's chest and my right under the body. Then I gave a heave, and over the fence went the horse."

Witnesses to the event are said to have corroborated Francisco's account, which was printed and reprinted in the newspapers of the time. Henry Clay, hearing the story for the first time from Peter, apparently enjoyed it. At the time, he was the target of political pamphleteers, and he jokingly told Peter that he was glad at least one member of the "pamphlet family" had been conquered.

Peter could certainly deal with adversaries with fierceness when the occasion warranted; however, he had a kinder and gentler side to his nature. With his friends, he often used his tremendous strength as an overgrown puppy might. Here's a typical story.

## The Milk in the Springhouse

As Peter Francisco and two friends were returning from a day of fishing, they passed a neighbor's farm. Crocks filled with milk had just been set in a trough inside the springhouse to cool. The sight and sound of the cold spring water running through the trough made the hot, tired men thirsty, and the sight of the cool milk made them even thirstier. Unfortunately, they could see it through a small grating, but they couldn't reach it. There was no way to get a drink because the milk was in the springhouse and the door was locked.

While the others sighed, Peter declared, "No problem, boys. It'll be easy enough to get into the springhouse—after all, there's no floor." He went to the rear of the little shack, slipped his fingers under the wooden framework, strained his powerful muscles and tilted the whole building up high enough for his friends to crawl under. As soon as they were inside, he let the house down, trapping them.

Peter jogged off to find the farmer, shouting, "Thieves! Thieves are in your springhouse stealing your fresh milk!"

The farmer, alarmed and angry, raced to the springhouse, and there, sure enough, were the two fishermen, staring out pitifully from behind the grating. Before any bodily harm could be done, Francisco quickly explained the trick he had pulled on his friends, and everyone, including the farmer, burst into laughter.

# CHAPTER THIRTEEN

## AND HE LIVED AS HAPPILY EVER AFTER
## AS ANYONE COULD

From 1785 to 1790, Peter and Susannah Francisco lived in a log cabin in Charlotte County, Virginia, until Susannah died in 1790, leaving a son and a daughter. Soon after her death, Francisco moved to Cumberland County, where he had purchased five hundred acres on both sides of Dry Creek. For several years, Peter made a living at farming and blacksmithing.

Four years after Susannah's death, Peter married Catharine Brooke from Farmer's Hall on the Rappahannock River. Catharine had been a relative and friend of Susannah, and Peter met her during a visit to the Anderson home after Susannah's death. They lived at Locust Grove, which Susannah had willed to their surviving son.

Catharine and Peter had two sons and two daughters together, but Peter was widowed again when Catharine died in 1821. In 1823, two years after Catharine's death, Francisco married Mary Beverly Grymes, a niece of Virginia governor Edmund

Randolph. She was only thirty-one, just half Francisco's age, when they were married.

Peter's much younger wife apparently twisted the Hercules of the Revolution around her little finger. Even though Peter had always been perfectly happy in the role of a planter and country gentleman, Mary was bored in the country and begged him to move to lively Richmond, where she could join in the social life of the capital city. Meekly, Francisco gave in to her wishes and bought a home in the city.

## Lafayette Returns

When the Marquis de Lafayette revisited America, the two Revolutionary warriors were reunited.

In 1824, President James Monroe invited Lafayette to tour the United States, partly to instill the "spirit of 1776" in the next generation of Americans and partly to celebrate the nation's fiftieth anniversary. Lafayette arrived in New York on August 15, 1824, and was greeted by approximately thirty thousand people. An estimated fifty thousand cheered Lafayette as he rode a wagon drawn by four white horses to New York's city hall. People tossed flowers at him, and mothers brought their children for his blessing. Some six thousand people attended a ball in his honor. He began a thirteen-month tour through all twenty-four states. At many stops on this tour, he was received by the public with a hero's welcome, and many honors and monuments were presented to commemorate and memorialize the Marquis de Lafayette's visit.

The records indicate that Peter Francisco escorted Lafayette on the Virginia portion of his triumphal tour. It's not clear if Peter accompanied him every step of the way, but if he did, here is a partial list of the Virginia tour the two old friends shared:

> October 17—Lafayette visited Mount Vernon and George Washington's tomb
>
> October 18–19—Lafayette arrived by steamer in Petersburg, VA to visit Yorktown for festivities marking the 43rd anniversary of the battle
>
> October 19–22—Lafayette visited Williamsburg and the College of William & Mary.
>
> October 22—Lafayette arrived in Norfolk, Virginia via steamer from Petersburg and spent four days there and in Portsmouth.
>
> October 26—Arrived in Richmond on a steamer from Norfolk. Edgar Allan Poe was in the youth honor guard in Richmond that welcomed him when he arrived.
>
> November 4—Lafayette visited former President Thomas Jefferson at Monticello.
>
> November 8—Lafayette attended a public banquet at the University of Virginia in nearby Charlottesville.

Different cities celebrated in different ways. Some held parades or conducted an artillery salute. In some places, schoolchildren were brought to welcome the Marquis. Veterans from the war, some of whom were in their sixties and seventies, welcomed him, sometimes joining him for a meal. While touring Yorktown, he recognized and embraced James Armistead Lafayette, the free African American double-agent spy, who adopted his last name to honor the Marquis; the story of the event was reported by the *Richmond Enquirer*.

Following that triumphal tour, Peter settled back in their Richmond home with Mary, living on his own resources supplemented by his soldier's pension. In 1825, with the support of his friends Colonel Charles Yancey and Judge Peter Johnson, he was appointed sergeant-at-arms for the Virginia House of Delegates and served in that position until his death in 1831. Yancey said that Peter was "as remarkable in many particulars as any man in the nation, his war achievements, his great size and manly prowess has given him a name and character throughout the nation that is known by those who never saw him." Johnson, a judge and Revolutionary War veteran, said, "I have no doubt that he killed more of the British than any 10 men in the American army. If Francisco could eat gold dust, this Legislature ought to feed him on it." Although in his sixties, Peter still had his legendary strength and had no problem throwing people out the chamber door.

Peter Francisco left several firsthand accounts of his Revolutionary War service. These were mostly in the form of pension applications written in his later years when, like many Revolutionary veterans, the effects of old wounds and age made it difficult for him to support his family. His various accounts differed somewhat from one another and from the other published accounts as well.

The following is a transcript of a petition written by Peter Francisco on February 15, 1828, addressed to the Virginia legislature and the United States Congress. It is transcribed exactly as Francisco wrote it, with some additions or corrections made for clarity:

> To the Honourable the Speaker and the Honourable the Members of the House of Delegates and the Senate and Congress of the United States.
>
> Your petitioner Peter Francisco humbly represents that he engaged in the glorious War of the Revolution in 1777.

He was in the Battles of Brandywine and GermanTown and the storming of Stony Point and [was] the second man who scaled the walls of the fort, after which a charge was ordered to be made in which your petitioner received a bayonet wound of extraordinary magnitude through the lower abdomen. Your petitioner killed the man at the flag staff who held the bayonet upon which your petitioner charged.

Your petitioner assisted at the Mud Island Fort [Fort Mifflin] on the Delaware River which was bravely defended by Colo[nel Samuel] Smith now in the Senate of the United States. Your petitioner was also in the battle at Monmouth in which he was wounded by a musket ball in the right thigh, the effects of which your petitioner sensibly feels in his old age, at times, in rainy or inclement weather, so as to give him considerable pain when he attempts to walk.

Your petitioner was in many skirmishes about New York and Philadelphia under Colo[nel Daniel] Morgan.

Your petitioner then came on to Virginia and volunteer'd under Colo[nel William] Mayo of Powhatan County. He was present at General [Horatio] Gates's defeat battle of Camden, [South Carolina] after the battle had nearly subsided, he saved the life of his Colonel by killing an officer who he discovered was in act of taking the life of the Colonel, a few minutes after which your petitioner immediately run him through the body with his bayonet and killed him on the spot.

Your petitioner then mounted the horse of his adversary and rode through [British lieutenant colonel Banastre] Tarleton's cavalry making them believe he was a Tory, by crying out ["]Huzzah my brave boys, we have conquered the d--n rebels.["] Your petitioner after making his escape in this way, he got in with [illegible] exhausted with fatigue; finding the Coln. in this situation, he gave him the horse which he had taken to ride to Hillsborough—Coln. Mayo feeling grateful to your petitioner, by his word promised to your petitioner one thousand acres of land on Rich Land Creek in Kentucky, which land he never got, the title being defective.

Your petitioner again returned to Virginia and understanding that Lord Cornwallis with his army were advancing through the Southern States. He a second time volunteered his services under Capt. [Thomas] Watkins of Prince Edward County and was at the Battle of Guilford N.C. at the close of the action Colo. [William] Washington ordered a charge with his Dragoons on eight hundred of the British troops called by the King's or Queen's Guards who laid by, as a reserve to cut off the retreat of the militia, in this charge your petitioner received a wound in the thigh the whole length of the bayonet. He killed four of the enemy in the presence of Colo. Washington who was near him.

Sometime after your petitioner's return from the Battle of Guilford your petitioner fell in with nine of Tarleton's cavalry, a plundering party, at the house of a Mr. Ward in the County of Amelia, one of whom demanded of your petitioner his knee buckles, watch, etc. Your petitioner refused to comply with the demand and told him if he wanted them he must help himself to them. Your petitioner had no arms about him at that time, in order to secure the buckles the paymaster who was one of the party, put his sword under his arm and when he was in the act of taking off the buckles your petitioner drew his sword from under his arm and gave him a blow on the head, which killed him. Your petitioner killed two other of the company and called with a loud voice to our people, to come and help this petitioner to take them, they believing that our troops were near, which was not the case, went off in a fright, and your petitioner took possession of all their horses, except one on which the vidette was sitting. They were part of about 400 men who were on their way to Prince Edward Court House to destroy our Military stores which were deposited at that place.

Your petitioner has met with considerable losses. He has sustained a few years past, the loss of all his crop of tobacco by fire, his smoke house with a large quantity of bacon, etc. Your petitioner has been compelled to sell his land, and in his old age has become poor.

Your petitioner prays this Honourable House to grant him a section of public land for the support of himself and family, and such pecuniary compensation as many enable him and his family to live free from want. Your petitioner was always a sober man and for many years lived the life of an industrious farmer. Your faithful old soldier appeals to the justice and magnanimity of this Honourable House to make such provision for your old volunteer soldier as may be deemed reasonable.

February 15, 1828
Peter Francisco

In early 1831, Peter Francisco fell ill with an intestinal ailment, which was probably appendicitis. He suffered for three weeks before he died at an estimated age of seventy-one. When Lafayette was notified of his death, he was deeply moved and sent a letter of sympathy to Francisco's third wife. The Virginia legislature passed a resolution of regret, and virtually every prominent official of the state from the governor down attended the funeral service held in the General Assembly Hall.

On January 18, 1831, the *Richmond Enquirer* published a eulogy:

> Died on Sunday in this city, after a lingering indisposition, Peter Francisco, Esq. the Sergeant-at-Arms of the House of Delegates and a Revolutionary Soldier, celebrated for his extraordinary strength, his undaunted courage, and his brilliant feats. The House of Delegates have determined to pay him the honors of a Public Funeral, and to bury him with the honors of war. The House have accordingly adjourned until tomorrow. The Resolutions passed on this occasion, and the Encomiums that were paid to the old Soldier's memory, are detailed in our account of the Proceedings of the House.

Peter Francisco was buried with full military and Masonic honors at the Shockoe Hill Cemetery, Richmond, Virginia.

# CHAPTER FOURTEEN

## PETER'S LEGACY

It is often said that a man is never truly dead until he is forgotten. Peter Francisco was a genuine American hero whose reputation was widely known and honored in his lifetime. His memory is kept alive in paintings, monuments, postage stamps and landmarks across the country.

His house, Locust Grove, located between Dillwyn and Buckingham, Virginia, was constructed before 1794. As the Peter Francisco House, it was added to the National Register of Historic Places on March 16, 1972.

The Colonial Trees Grove in Golden Gate Park is a collection of historic trees that honor the original thirteen colonies of Delaware, Pennsylvania, New York, New Jersey, Connecticut, Georgia, Maryland, Massachusetts, Georgia, Virginia, South Carolina, North Carolina and Rhode Island. The grove dates back to 1896, when the San Francisco Chapter of the National Society of Daughters of the American Revolution (DAR) began to collect and plant the specimens. Every tree represents a different species native to the location it symbolizes, each with soil from a soldier's grave. There, at the park, stands a chestnut tree with soil from Peter Francisco's grave.

In addition to Peter Francisco Square in New Bedford, Massachusetts, there are several monuments. They stand in Rhode Island; Guilford Courthouse, North Carolina; the Ironbound section of Newark, New Jersey; and Hopewell, Virginia.

Since 1953, March 15 has been officially recognized in Massachusetts, Rhode Island and Virginia as Peter Francisco Day. He is the only enlisted man from the Revolutionary War to be honored in this way.

There may even have been a poem written about him. "Black Samson of Brandywine" by Paul Laurence Dunbar, in *The Complete Poems of Paul Laurence Dunbar* (New York: Dodd, Mead, and Company, 1913), seems to have been inspired by his reputation. Although Peter was not "black as the pinions of night," nor did he swing a scythe, it's hard not to recognize the parallels in this poem, published 136 years after the Battle of Brandywine. By all accounts, Peter had a swarthy complexion, no doubt darkened by the sun, and he certainly cut a giant figure. Though he didn't have his broadsword at Brandywine, it may have been that sword that Dunbar refers to as a scythe (or perhaps it refers to the scythe of the Grim Reaper).

"Black Samson of Brandywine"
by Paul Laurence Dunbar

Gray are the pages of record,
Dim are the volumes of eld;
Else had old Delaware told us
More that her history held.

Told us with pride in the story,
Honest and noble and fine,
More of the tale of my hero,
Black Samson of Brandywine.
Sing of your chiefs and your nobles,
Saxon and Celt and Gaul,
Breath of mine ever shall join you,
Highly I honor them all.
Give to them all of their glory,
But for this noble of mine,
Lend him a tithe of your tribute,
Black Samson of Brandywine.
There in the heat of the battle,
There in the stir of the fight,
Loomed he, an ebony giant,
Black as the pinions of night.
Swinging his scythe like a mower
Over a field of grain,
Needless the care of the gleaners,
Where he had passed amain.
Straight through the human harvest,
Cutting a bloody swath,
Woe to you, soldier of Briton!
Death is abroad in his path.
Flee from the scythe of the reaper,
Flee while the moment is thine,
None may with safety withstand him,
Black Samson of Brandywine.
Was he a freeman or bondman?
Was he a man or a thing?
What does it matter? His brav'ry
Renders him royal—a king.

If he was only a chattel,
Honor the ransom may pay
Of the royal, the loyal black giant
Who fought for his country that day.
Noble and bright is the story,
Worthy the touch of the lyre,
Sculptor or poet should find it
Full of the stuff to inspire.
Beat it in brass and in copper,
Tell it in storied line,
So that the world may remember
Black Samson of Brandywine.

Whether the poem refers to Peter or not, he is well represented in literature. There have been several historical fiction books written about him in addition to the nonfiction newspaper, book and journal articles mentioned in the resource list. For an exciting, larger-than-life account, read Travis Bowman's *Hercules of the Revolution: A Novel Based on the Life of Peter Francisco* (n.p.: Bequest Publishing, 2009). Mr. Bowman is a seventh-generation descendant of Peter Francisco who stands six feet, six inches tall just like his famous ancestor. In 2008, he began live performances of Peter's story, using a six-foot replica broadsword, and in 2010, he produced the first television documentary about Peter Francisco called *The Peter Francisco Story*. He is working on a movie based on his novel, which he expects to see released in 2015.

In 1975, the United States Postal Services issued a "Peter Francisco, Fighter Extraordinary" U.S. postage stamp as part of the Contributors to the Cause series.

## SO NOW YOU'VE HEARD OF PETER FRANCISCO!

It's easy to understand why Peter was called the Hercules of the American Revolution, the Virginia Giant, a One-Man Army. Through battle after battle, injury after injury and hardship after hardship, he demonstrated the true meaning of heroism.

Peter's legacy lives on—not so much in the stone monuments or the written words as in his inspiring example of loyalty, perseverance and courage. Peter Francisco may not have been a superhero, but he was a super American.

# GLOSSARY AND PRONUNCIATION GUIDE

*(Definitions based on* Encarta Dictionary*)*

**abatis** (ah-buh-tiz): a rampart made from felled trees. They were slanted in shape and sharp to the touch. The cut branches were laid at a small distance from a trench or ditch, pointing outward, with the butts fastened to the ground so that they could not be removed.

**artificer** (ar-tif-i-ser): a person whose work requires manual skill, such as a blacksmith, carpenter or saddle maker

**artillery**: cannons; these fired heavy metal balls that smashed fortifications, ships and soldiers. "Artillery" also refers to the soldiers who fire the cannons.

**artillery salute**: firing cannons as a military display of honor

**bastions**: fortified places

**battalion**: a military unit usually including headquarters plus three or more smaller units (batteries or squads)

**battery**: a group of artillery pieces functioning as a single unit

**bayonet**: a blade attached to the end of the musket, used for stabbing

**bombard**: attack or hit repeatedly

**bombs**: hollow spheres cast of iron. The wall of the sphere contained a small hole through which gunpowder would be poured and then into which a fuse would be stuck and lit.

**boycott**: to refuse to take part in something as a means of protest

**breeches** (britch-ez): knee-length pants

**brigade**: two or more battalions or regiments

**broadside**: a large sheet of paper printed on only one side (poster) announcing events or public statements

**campaign**: a series of operations in one area intended to achieve a specific objective

**causeway**: a raised path or road over a marsh or water

**cavalry**: soldiers on horseback

**Chief Oskanondohna** (ahs-kah-nahn-donna)

**colonists**: residents of the American colonies

**colors cased**: flags tightly furled or covered

**commission**: an appointment to the rank of officer

**concourse**: a large space where people can gather in a public place or building

**conscript**: to force people to join the army

**corps**: a military force that carries out specialized duties

**currency**: money

**delegates**: people chosen to represent or act on behalf of a group

**detachments**: a group of soldiers separated from the larger unit for special duties

**diversionary tactic**: an action designed to distract or delay the enemy

**division**: a military unit capable of sustained operations, including a headquarters and two or more brigades

**dragoons**: a heavily armed soldier on horseback

**dressing the line**: to form a close-knit line, fire, kneel and reload as the next line moves forward to fire

**enlist**: to voluntarily join the military

**entrenchment**: a defensive ditch or trench

**evacuate**: to make everyone leave a place

**fife**: a small, high-pitched flute without keys

**firelock**: the mechanism that struck a spark from flint and caused a charge to explode

**flint**: a spark-making rock

**ford**: a crossing place through shallow water

**fortify**: to make a place stronger against attack

**frizzen**: historically called the steel, the frizzen is an L-shaped piece of steel hinged at the rear used in a musket

**gauling** (another spelling for galling) **fire**: frustrating, distracting or irritating the enemy by firing weapons

**gill**: a unit of liquid measure equal to a half cup (four ounces)

**grenade**: a small bomb that is thrown by hand

**grenadier**: a tall, strong soldier, probably armed with grenades

**grievances**: reasons for complaint

**ground arms**: to pile or stack military weapons on the ground

**guerrilla** (guh-rill-uh): soldiers operating in small groups to harass or carry out sabotage

**harrying**: pestering, annoying or hassling

**haversack**: a strong bag carried on the back or shoulder

**Hercules**: in Roman mythology, he was the son of Jupiter and Alcmene, noted for his courage and great strength

**hogshead**: a large barrel that could hold sixty-three gallons of liquid or dry goods

**indentured servant**: an immigrant to North America between the seventeenth and eighteenth centuries who contracted to work for an employer for a number of years in exchange for accommodation

**infantrymen**: foot soldiers

**lashes**: strokes with a whip

**legion**: a large military unit

**legislature**: the part of the government that makes or changes laws

**light infantry**: soldiers whose job was to provide a screen ahead of the main body of infantry, harassing and delaying the enemy advance.

**magazine**: storehouse for military supplies

**marquee** (mar-ki): a large tent

**marquis** (mar-ki): a nobleman ranking above a count

**militia** (muh-lish-uh): an army of soldiers who are civilians but take military training and serve full time during emergencies

**musket**: a shoulder gun with a long barrel and smooth bore

**musketeers**: infantrymen armed with muskets

**nom de guerre** (nom-duh-ger): an assumed name that somebody uses when fighting

**Oneida** (own-eye-da): Native American Iroquoian people

**palisade**: a fence made of pointed slats of wood (pales) driven into the ground for defense

**pamphleteers**: people who write opinion-filled pamphlets

**parade**: same as parade ground: area where troops gather in formation for inspection or training

**parapet**: protective walls of earth piled up along the edge of a military trench for protection from enemy fire

**parley**: to talk or negotiate with an enemy

**parliament**: group of people who make the laws and run the government in Great Britain and other countries

**pension**: money paid to a person no longer serving in the army

**picket** (or picquett): soldier or soldiers on guard

**planter**: wealthy farmer

**profiteering**: making excessive profits by charging high prices for scarce, necessary or rationed goods

**Prussia**: the former largest state of Germany

**Pyrrhic victory**: a victory won at such a great cost to the victor that it is the same as defeat

**rebellion**: a struggle against the people in charge of a government

**reconnoiter**: to explore to gather information

**recruit**: to ask someone to join the military

**regiment**: a military unit usually consisting or two or three battalions under the command of a colonel

**rendezvous** (rahn-day-voo): to bring people together at an agreed time and place

**repeal**: to officially withdraw or cancel a law or legal decision

**reveille** (rev-uh-lee): the sounding of the bugle to awaken and summon military personnel in a camp

**sally port**: an opening in a fortification from which defenders can spring out suddenly (make sallies)

**Schuylkill River** (skoo-kill): the 128-mile river in Pennsylvania

**seize**: to take possession of a city or area

**siege** (see-dj): a military operation in which troops surround a place and cut off all outside access in order to force surrender

**suite**: group of followers and advisors accompanying someone very important

**tattoo**: a steady, rhythmic drumbeat

**tax**: money collected from a country's citizens to help pay for running the government

**Tidewater**: the coastal region of eastern Virginia

**timbrel**: a tambourine or small hand drum

**Tory**: a resident of the American colonies who supported the British

**treason**: the crime of betraying one's own country

**Viscount de Noailles** (vai-count duh no-ay): a viscount is the son or younger brother of a count

**volley**: simultaneous firing of several weapons

**Von Steuben** (von stoo-ben)

# TIMELINE OF THE REVOLUTION
# AND PETER'S LIFE

*Entries about Peter's life appear in italics*

| | |
|---|---|
| 1760 | *Peter Francisco may have been born on July 9 in Porto Judeu on Terceira, Portuguese-held Azores, to father Machado Luiz Francisco and mother Antonia Maria* |
| 1764 | Sugar Act and Currency Act |
| 1765 | Quartering Act and Stamp Act<br>*Peter abducted or sent away from his family*<br>*Peter found on a wharf on June 23 in City Point, Virginia; eventually taken in by Judge Winston* |
| 1766 | Repeal of Stamp Act |
| 1767 | Townshend Acts |
| 1770 | Boston Massacre; five people are killed |

| | |
|---|---|
| 1773 | Tea Act<br>Boston Tea Party |
| 1774 | First Continental Congress<br>First Virginia Convention |
| 1775 | Lexington and Concord<br>Second Continental Congress<br>George Washington named commander in chief<br>Battle of Bunker Hill (neither side won)<br>Second Virginia Congress |
| 1776 | Declaration of Independence adopted and signed<br>Battle of Long Island, New York (British victory)<br>Battle of White Plains, New York (British victory)<br>Battle of Trenton, New Jersey (American victory)<br>Benjamin Franklin convinced France to secretly support<br>    the war effort<br>*Peter joined the Continental army* |
| 1777 | Battle of Princeton, New Jersey (American victory)<br>Battle of Saratoga, New York (American victory)<br>Siege of Ticonderoga, New York (British victory)<br>First American flag sewn by Betsy Ross, possibly at George<br>    Washington's request<br>*Battle of Brandywine Creek, Pennsylvania* (British victory);<br>    *Peter wounded*<br>*Battle of Germantown, Pennsylvania* (British victory)<br>*Defense of Fort Mifflin, Pennsylvania* (British victory)<br>*Winter at Valley Forge* |

| | |
|---|---|
| 1778 | France and America officially became allies |
| | *Battle of Monmouth, New Jersey* (neither side won); *Peter wounded* |
| 1779 | British attacked in both North and South |
| | *Battle of Stony Point, New York* (American victory); *Peter wounded* |
| | *Battle of Paulus Hook, New Jersey* (American victory) |
| | Siege of Savannah, Georgia |
| 1780 | British take Charleston, South Carolina |
| | *Battle of Camden, North Carolina* (British victory) |
| | *Battle of Kings Mountain, South Carolina* (American victory) |
| | *Battle of Guilford Courthouse, North Carolina* (British Pyrrhic victory); *Peter wounded* |
| 1781 | *Battle of Yorktown, Virginia* (American victory) |
| | Cornwallis surrendered |
| 1782 | Peace negotiations began in France |
| | *Peter learned to read and write* |
| 1783 | The United States and Great Britain signed the Treaty of Paris, officially ending the war |
| 1812 | War of 1812 began |
| 1824 | Lafayette returned to America; *Peter joined him on tour of Virginia* |
| 1831 | *Peter died of appendicitis; buried in Shockoe Cemetery, Richmond, Virginia* |

# WHERE TO LEARN MORE: STUDENT RESOURCES

Beller, Susan Borost. *Yankee Doodle and the Redcoats: Soldiering in the Revolutionary War*. Soldiers on the Battlefront. Minneapolis, MN: Twenty-first Century Books, 2008.

Freedman, David. *Give Me Liberty: The Story of the Declaration of Independence*. New York: Holiday House, 2000.

"The History Place: Prelude to Revolution. American Revolution 1763–1775." The History Place. www.historyplace.com/unitedstates/revolution/rev-prel.htm.

Huey, Lois Miney. *Voices of the American Revolution: Stories from the Battlefields*. Mankato, MN: Capstone Press, 2011.

Murray, Stuart. *American Revolution*. Eyewitness Books. New York: DK Publishers, Inc., 2002.

Ratliff, Thomas M. *How to Be a Revolutionary War Soldier*. Washington, D.C.: National Geographic Children's Books, 2008.

Raum, Elizabeth. *The Revolutionary War: An Interactive Adventure*. Mankato, MN: Capstone Press, 2010.

Redmond, Shirley Raye. *Patriots in Petticoats: Heroines of the American Revolution*. New York: Random House, 2004.

# WORKS CITED

American Revolution. National Park Service. www.nps.gov/
revwar. Accessed August 2013.

*American Scene: Events.* Vol. 2: *A New Nation Emerges: 1776–
1828.* Danbury, CT: Grolier, 1999.

Bailey, James. H. *Peter Francisco: Washington's One-Man
Regiment.* Manuscript, circa 1940.

Bigelow, Barbara, and Linda Schmittroth. *American Revolution:
Almanac.* Detroit, MI: UXL, 2000.

Bissell, Richard. *New Light on 1776 and All That.* Boston: Little,
Brown, 1975.

"The British Surrender at Yorktown, 1781." Eyewitness to History.
www.eyewitnesstohistory.com/yorktown.htm. Accessed November
2013.

"Colonial Trees Grove." Golden Gate Park. www.golden-gate-
park.com/colonial-trees-grove.html. Accessed October 2013.

Cook, Fred J. *What Manner of Men: Forgotten Heroes of the
American Revolution.* New York: William Morrow & Co., 1959.

Crews, Ed. "Hercules of the American Revolution: Peter Francisco." *Colonial Williamsburg* 28, no. 4 (Autumn 2006): 20–25.

Dolan, Edward F. *The American Revolution: How We Fought the War of Independence.* Brockfield, CT: Millbrook Press, 1995.

"Final Payment Vouchers for Military Pensions." Fold3 History and Genealogy Archives. www.footnotelibrary. com/s.php#query=peter+francisco&preview=1 &t=886,823,450,851,854,784,891,654,895,761,875,876. Accessed November 2013.

Freedman, David. *Give Me Liberty: The Story of the Declaration of Independence.* New York: Holiday House, 2000.

George, Lynn. *A Timeline of the American Revolution.* New York: Rosen Publishing, 2003.

Gustaitis, Joseph. "One-Man Army." *American History* 29, no. 4 (1994): 56+.

Hamilton, Charles Henry. *Peter Francisco, Soldier Extraordinaire: Most Famous Private Soldier of the Revolutionary War.* Richmond, VA: Whittet & Shepperson, 1976.

Huey, Lois Miney. *Voices of the American Revolution: Stories from the Battlefields.* Mankato, MN: Capstone Press, 2011.

Kelly, C. Brian, with Ingrid Smyer. *Best Little Stories from the American Revolution: More Than 100 True Stories.* 2nd ed. Naperville, IL: Cumberland House, 2011.

Lloyd, Sandy. "Valley Forge—Varnum's HQ: The Portuguese Giant—Peter Francisco." A living history script. Philadelphia: Historic Philadelphia, Inc., 2009.

Mauldin, Bill. *Mud & Guts: A Look at the Common Soldier of the American Revolution.* Harpers Ferry, WV: Division of Publications, National Park Service, U.S. Dept. of the Interior, 1978.

Murphy, Daniel P. *The Everything American Revolution Book, from the Boston Massacre to the Campaign at Yorktown—All*

*You Need to Know About the Birth of Our Country*. Avon, MA: Adams Media, 2008.

Murray, Stuart. *American Revolution*. Eyewitness Books. New York: DK Publishers, Inc., 2002.

National Park Service. *The American Revolution: Official Park Service Handbook*. Fort Washington, PA: Eastern National, 2008. Available from eparks, the Official Online Store of America's National Parks. www.eparks.com/store/product/68008/The-American-Revolution%3A-Official-National-Park-Service-Handbook. Accessed August 2013.

"Patriotic Verse in a Schoolboy's Math Book during the Revolutionary War." The Gilder Lehrman Institute of American History. www.gilderlehrman.org/collections/treasures-from-the-collection/patriotic-verse-schoolboy%E2%80%99s-math-book-during-revolutionary. Accessed December 2013.

"Peter Francisco 1820 petition to Virginia Assembly." *William and Mary College Quarterly Historical Magazine*. books.google.com/books?id=WtURAAAAYAAJ&pg=PA217&dq=Peter+Francisco+1820+petition+to+Virginia+Assembly&hl=en&ei=0rixTNSxBYyMnQe60pyUBg&sa=X&oi=book_result&ct=result&resnum=2&ved=0CC0Q6AEwAQ#v=onepage&q=Peter%20Francisco%201820%20petition%20to%20Virginia%20Assembly&f=false. Accessed August 2013.

*Peter Francisco: Remarkable American Revolutionary War Soldier*. Originally published by *American History* magazine. Published online June 12, 2006, at www.historynet.com/?s=Peter+Francisco&=. Accessed October 2013.

"Polly Cooper: Oneida Heroine." Oneida Indian Nation. www.oneidaindiannation.com/history/noteworthyoneidas/39567117.html. Accessed August 2013.

Ratliff, Thomas M. *How to Be a Revolutionary War Soldier.* Washington, D.C.: National Geographic Children's Books, 2008.

Redmond, Shirley Raye. *Patriots in Petticoats: Heroines of the American Revolution.* New York: Random House, 2004.

Rees, John U. "'We are now...properly...enwigwamed.' British Soldiers and Brush Shelters, 1777–1781." Published in the *Brigade Dispatch* (Journal of the Brigade of the American Revolution) 29, no. 2 (Summer 1999): 2–9. revwar75.com/library/rees/enwigwamed.htm. Accessed November 2013.

Shippey, D.H.T., and Michael Burns. "Giant." Parts One and Two. *Breeds Hill Gazette*, September and October 2011. www.breedshill.org/The_Breeds_Hill_institute/Giant.html.

"Soldier Stories." Army Heritage Center Foundation. www.armyheritage.org/education-and-programs/educational-resources/soldier-stories/281-revwarequipment.html. Accessed February 25, 2013.

Truex, Mark. "The Virginia Hercules." A research paper, 2013.

Valley Forge. National Park Service. www.nps.gov/vafo/index.htm. Accessed August 24, 2013.

Ward, Harry M. *For Virginia and for Independence: Twenty-eight Revolutionary War Soldiers from the Old Dominion Continental Infantry.* Jefferson, NC: MacFarland & Co., 2011.

"Washington, George, 1732–1799." Biographical Directory of the United Sates Congress. bioguide.congress.gov/scripts/guidedisplay.pl?index=w000178. Accessed November 2013.

Yeck, Joanne L. *At a Place Called Buckingham: Historic Sketches of Buckingham County, Virginia.* Dayton, OH: Greyden Press, 2011.

# ABOUT THE AUTHORS

**SHERRY NORFOLK** is an award-winning, internationally acclaimed storyteller and teaching artist, performing and leading residencies and professional development workshops across the United States and Southeast Asia. Co-author of *Literacy Development in the Storytelling Classroom* (Westport, CT: Libraries Unlimited, 2009), *The Storytelling Classroom: Applications Across the Curriculum* (Westport, CT: Libraries Unlimited, 2006) and *Social Studies in the Storytelling Classroom* (Little Rock, AR: Parkhurst Brothers Publishing, 2012), she is a leading authority on integrating learning through storytelling. She also co-authored *The Moral of the Story: Folktales for Character Development* and six picture books. Sherry received the National Storytelling Network Oracle Award for Distinguished National Service, as well as Tennessee Arts

Commission's Outstanding Teaching Artist of 2010 award. She serves as adjunct professor in the Creative Arts in Learning program at Lesley University and was one of thirty teaching artists chosen to attend the first National Seminar for Teaching Artists, developed and hosted by the Kennedy Center for the Performing Arts. Visit her website at www.sherrynorfolk.com.

**BOBBY NORFOLK**, an internationally known story performer and teaching artist, is a three-time Emmy Award winner and Parents' Choice honoree. One of the most popular and dynamic story-educators in America today, Bobby was given the national Circle of Excellence Oracle Award, an honor presented by the National Storytelling Network, which recognizes the very best storytellers in the nation. This prestigious award is given to artists who set the standard of excellence in their craft for exceptional commitment and exemplary contributions to the art of storytelling.

Bobby has created over ten CDs, many having won the prestigious Parents Choice Gold Award. He has co-authored eight children's books and won first prize from *Foreword Magazine* in the Spoken Word category with his *Dunbar Outloud* CD. His book *The Moral of the Story: Folktales for Character Development* is a popular reference handbook for using story in the classroom. He is also a contributing author in *Writer's Choice* (New York: McGraw-Hill/Glencoe Press 1999); *The Storytelling Classroom: Applications Across the Curriculum* (Westport, CT: Libraries Unlimited, 2006); *Social Studies in the Storytelling Classroom* (Little Rock, AR; Parkhurst Brothers

Publishing, 2012); and *Literacy Development in the Storytelling Classroom* (Westport, CT: Libraries Unlimited, 2009.)

Bobby travels both nationally and internationally presenting performances, keynotes and workshops. A past member of the board of directors for the National Storytelling Network, he currently serves on the St. Louis Storytelling Festival Advisory Council and is a featured artist in festivals worldwide. He founded Folktale Productions, a storytelling company, in 1987. His website is www.bobbynorfolk.com.